# THE DWELLING PLACE OF WONDER

# THE DWELLING PLACE OF WONDER

Harry L. Serio

RESOURCE *Publications* · Eugene, Oregon

THE DWELLING PLACE OF WONDER

Copyright © 2016 Harry L. Serio. All rights reserved. Except for brief quotations in critical publications or reviews, no part of this book may be reproduced in any manner without prior written permission from the publisher. Write: Permissions, Wipf and Stock Publishers, 199 W. 8th Ave., Suite 3, Eugene, OR 97401.

Resource Publications
An Imprint of Wipf and Stock Publishers
199 W. 8th Ave., Suite 3
Eugene, OR 97401

www.wipfandstock.com

PAPERBACK ISBN: 978-1-4982-9157-6
HARDCOVER ISBN: 978-1-4982-9159-0
EBOOK ISBN: 978-1-4982-9158-3

Manufactured in the U.S.A.

# THE DWELLING PLACE OF WONDER

*Preface* | vii

The Play Is Memory | 1
Present at the Creation | 4
Familia | 6
Table of Memories | 10
The Farmer from Saratov | 14
The Mad Monk | 20
Among the Gladiators | 24
The Sunshine Hook | 28
The Rolling Gardens of Pacific Street | 32
Renaissance Man | 35
Aunt Bette | 39
Billy | 43
The Rat Safari | 45
Saturday Matinee at the Rivoli | 47
The Restorer of Souls | 51
"Hello Darkness, My Old Friend" | 54
Newspapers | 57
Eyes on the Steeple | 60
The Church of the Vanishing Jesus | 65
It Started with a Coffee Can | 69

## THE DWELLING PLACE OF WONDER

The Oak in Independence Park | 71
The Magic Sandbox | 75
A Friend from Lithuania | 80
Circumambulating the Marne | 84
Holocaust | 89
The Crone | 98
Banana Bob Sleeps with the Fishes | 101
Chasing Gypsies | 104
Angels Descending | 111
Butterfly Wings | 115
Wordsworth Williams | 120
Ghosts | 123
A Trickle of Blood in the Gutter | 125
Walking the Goat | 129
Murder in the Morning | 131
Memories of Cats and Other Strangers | 136
Passing Ships | 138
"I Will Always Have Paris" | 141
The Gloaming | 146
On Bradley Creek | 151
The Dwelling Place of Wonder | 155

# PREFACE

I AM NOT CERTAIN whether in some pre-existent state I made the decision to enter this life and confront all the variables that determine one's course through all the years of living. Did I pre-select my parents or where I would be born or the world in which I would live? Were the events that filled my earlier years somehow chosen in order to lead me in a particular direction and to shape who I would become?

Life is not accidental, but it is nevertheless filled with events that astonish and amaze as well as the ordinary routines that everyone moves through. Heredity, environment, relationships, and so many other factors add to the beauty and wonder of life. Ralph Waldo Emerson was right when he observed, "Evermore in the world is this marvelous balance of beauty and disgust, magnificence and rats."

What I have written in this book are some of the events that have given meaning and texture to my life. Every time I revisit my past I find new meaning in what has occurred. We are always in the process of becoming, and continual reflection contributes to that process. The past is indeed a dwelling place of wonder.

I am grateful to many people whose lives have intersected with my own in meaningful ways—family, friends, associates, parishioners, and those with whom brief encounters have also influenced and changed the direction of my life. I owe much to them—in particular to my wife, Mary Ann, and children (Stuart, Tasha, and Matthew). I also appreciate the contributions of friends and colleagues who read this manuscript, made helpful suggestions, and offered encouragement, especially Maren Tirabassi, John Morgan, Byron Borger, and Mary Ann Serio.

The journey continues and every event is meaningful and filled with purpose and wonder.

# THE PLAY IS MEMORY

WE CREATE THE WORLDS we inhabit.

I can sit on my swing in the backyard and look toward the line of trees two hundred feet away. Squirrels cavort nearby. Birds eat out of our feeders. Groundhogs scurry around the fringes of our property. They are part of my world as I observe and think about this one-acre universe of my perception.

I could narrow my field of vision to the bit of grass at my feet and see in miniature a tangled environment of various strains of grass, twigs, stones, and seed pods—rugged terrain for the insects that crawl about or hover slightly above. If I look no farther than this patch of turf and allow it to be my world, it becomes a vast plain inhabited by thousands of life forms, some so small as to be barely perceptible to the human eye.

Though I cannot see it, I know that there are an infinite number of microscopic worlds around me with billions and billions of micro-organisms living and dying within their own life cycles.

The silence of my world is penetrated by the distant sounds of laughter coming from beyond the trees. Though I cannot see what is happening, I recognize the sounds as human, and with the sound of splashing water I deduce that there is a pool party going on. My senses now incorporate a larger world. The neighbor's dog barking expands my world in another direction. My short-term memory gathers these divergent sensory stimuli and my mind creates the world that I am experiencing.

I can probe other memory banks to recall conversations I had earlier in the day, the trip to Philadelphia yesterday, a conference I attended last week, people I had known a decade ago, an incident from childhood.

A television series in the eighties, *St. Elsewhere*—a medical drama set amid the staff of a Boston hospital—had a unique ending to its final season.

# THE DWELLING PLACE OF WONDER

It was revealed at the conclusion that all of the episodes were fragments in the impenetrable mind of an autistic child. It was the writer's way of saying that all is illusion, that we create our own worlds, our own separate realities, and then we determine how we will react to the perception of the events around us. I create my world new every day, and then re-create it.

Is my world only what I experience at the moment or is it the accumulated memories of a lifetime? Are the lives we live no more than memory and illusion and interpretation? Of course they are all, for as Anaïs Nin has said, "We see life, not as it is, but as we are."

The novelist Anne Sexton once said that it didn't matter who her father was. What mattered was how she remembered him. Perhaps Woody Allen said it better in his film, *Deconstructing Harry*: "We all know the same truth. Our lives consist of how we choose to distort it."

Our lives are shaped by the experiences of our past. Not so much by what has happened to us, but by how we continually remember those experiences and perpetually revise them in the replaying. The Apostle Paul may have put away childish things, and we may put the past behind us, but we never stop learning from who we were and what we did. The events of our lives continually reshape our present and our future. The child is indeed father to the man.

Tennessee Williams in his autobiographical play, "The Glass Menagerie," has the narrator, Tom Wingfield, open with these words: "The play is memory. Being a memory play, it is dimly lighted, it is sentimental, it is not realistic."

How we remember our past shapes our reality, our perspective, our framework for understanding persons and events. Our lives are a work in progress, and we are continually rewriting the script. I imagine heaven to be a wonderful welcoming party where I will be greeted by those I've known in life who have gone before me, as well as by familiar persons whom I have never known in this life. As we sit down at the banquet table, they will gather about and ask, "So, what did you learn?"

What I do in life is never as important as what I learn from it. And if I learn my lessons well and become a better person because of them, I will have been a blessing to others in their journeys.

What I have written is memory—a life not necessarily as I have lived it, but as I have remembered it. I have spent my days slipping over the surface of life, seldom probing its depths. I have learned a little about everything, but never quite gaining the wisdom that comes from living out the true

## THE PLAY IS MEMORY

essence of one's being. Like an old phonograph needle that skims across a plastic landscape producing only endless sounds, I have not valued the ups and downs, the peaks and valleys of life. Yet, it is on the slopes and depths that the music is heard. It simply took a lifetime to play it back and hear it.

I have created my world and tinted the windows through which I view it. These are my memories, my baggage, my junk. No one can say it isn't so, for they would only be replacing my world with their own.

# PRESENT AT THE CREATION

I WAS BORN AT an early age, and so I have difficulty remembering the day I emerged into this world. I don't recall whether that September morning was a bright, sunny day that would be an indication, true or not, of the life to follow, or if it was a gray dawn that would mark a cloudy future.

Sometimes I think I remember the day, or at least my departure from the other side, the realm of the spirit. There is a legend that assumes the pre-existence of the soul and that at the moment of entry into this life, an angel puts her finger to the formless lips of the child-to-be and says simply, "Forget."

There is then no longer a conscious awareness of the former existence until the return following death. There are only fragments of memory, a feeling that there is more to life than what we observe, some fleeting moments of yearning for what had been in another time, another existence, perhaps even in another state of being.

Lurking somewhere in the primal consciousness that begins developing in the cerebral cortex of the embryotic brain are the faint traces of that memory of a previous existence. It is that element that leads to religious constructs to explain who we are, where we have come from, how we can maintain contact with our spiritual origins, and what our purpose and our destiny might be.

A group of early Christians known as the *pre-existiani* believed that the souls of all persons existed before they were born. The early church theologian Origen shared this belief, and it was later perpetuated among the Albigenses who further developed the concept of Christian reincarnationism. Although Origen was condemned by the church at the Second

# PRESENT AT THE CREATION

Council of Constantinople in 553, his beliefs continued as an expression of Christian mysticism.

My own belief is that I have entered this life with a purpose, and that my experiences—a combination of events, feelings, relationships, knowledge, and wisdom—all are part of why I am here. I am less certain as to why this purpose exists, whether for my eternal spiritual growth, or for some aggregate spiritual entity or collective unconsciousness in whom resides the totality of all that is and has been and is to be, and of which I am ultimately a part.

Nevertheless, I feel that there is a divine spark within me, a manifestation of the divine, the Christ-essence if you will, that makes me at one with all living creatures and spiritual entities on this planet and those that may exist throughout the universe.

If this sounds "esoteric," that's OK, because we are all "out of this world," which is what *esoteric* literally means. We have our origins beyond the realm of time and space. What I have written, however, is a narrative of this temporal existence and my attempt to make sense out of my own life, those who are a part of it, and those who have skirted the edges of it bringing their own gifts of insight to my life.

# FAMILIA

Genealogies tend to be boring. Only very few people are interested in the family trees of others, unless they happen to be a monarch, president, or someone of great renown. The writer of Matthew's gospel includes the genealogy of Jesus, which contains some very notable celebrities of the Bible. It also contains some rather seedy characters that could embarrass some descendants.

Included among Jesus' ancestors are Abraham, who put his own wife at risk in order to save himself; Jacob, who lied and cheated his brother out of his birthright; Tamar, a prostitute who fornicated with her father-in-law to produce a child; Rahab, a Canaanite spy and prostitute; Ruth, a foreigner, who had a questionable encounter with Boaz after he got drunk; David, an adulterer, who had Bathsheba's husband placed in the front line of battle to cover up his sin; and Solomon, who had three hundred concubines and worshipped Astarte, the Phoenician goddess of love and fertility. With such a background it is no wonder that the church emphasized the virgin birth of Jesus.

My own family probably has its own cast of colorful characters. I have learned that my father's family descended from an old and distinguished Italian line that traces its origins to the nobility of Naples. A genealogy requested by my cousin, Don Ciro Maria Serio, a priest in the town of Nocera Inferiore where many of the Serios lived, gives this brief history:

> The Serios belong among the noble families of Naples. A branch was joined to the patrician family of Ostuni (Lecce) resulting, in the 18th century, in the births of Antonio and Ludovico Serio in Vicolo Equense in 1748. Ludovico was an extemporaneous poet from 1771. He was a professor of eloquent Italian at the University

of Naples. He died fighting on the banks of the Sebeto (a little river of the Campania region which feeds into the Gulf of Naples). The battle pitted the Neopolitan soldiers defending the Holy Faith against the followers of the Partenopean Republic.

Various members of the House of Serio held power in the Reign of the Two Sicilies (*Regno delle due Sicilie*) under Ferdinand IV in 1854. The Serio family flourished and enjoyed nobility in Sicily as well as Naples.

The brevity of this description has led me to speculate on who was left out of the family tree and why. In 1955, Don Ciro requested the *Instituto Genealogico Italiano* to research the Serio family crest. They provided gratis the following description:

> The antique helmet is placed on the shield as a remembrance of the cavalier, the military tasks, and also the expeditions to the Holy Land. The crown is that of nobility because the Serio had this distinction. The lion is the most noble animal of heraldry. The symbol represented the Command, the Grandeur, and Magnanimity. The lion holding the compass is showing the council of the strong and just man, the profound courage and knowledge of the world. The stars are configured to indicate the brightness of the future heirs. The undulating patterns are generally emblematic of the course of water and of the ocean waves.
>
> The crest symbolizes the River Serio (a river of the province of Bergamo which feeds the Adda and subsequently joins the Po and with these feeds the Gulf of Venice and then the Adriatic Sea) and represents the meaning spoken by the name Serio.

The information was obtained from the original framed crest owned by Fr. Ciro. Since his death, the crest is in possession of his niece, Maria Picaro, in Nocera Inferiore. In the 1980's, Emilio Serio, working from a photograph of the crest and a heraldric description, painted the Serio family crest that was distributed to the New Jersey clan of Luigi Serio.

There is something ironic about the children of poor immigrants displaying an icon of lost nobility and the faded grandeur of past history when they have achieved their own success and placed their own stamp on the heritage they will pass on to their children.

In the new science of epigenetics there is evidence that the life experiences of parents can affect the genetic character of their children so that behavioral traits can be passed down through generations. It may also explain cultural memory, the retention of habits and traditions, as well as the Jungian concept of racial memory. We do inherit more than we think we do from our ancestors.

Today, Serios can be found in abundance in both Campania and Sicily, which appears to be their prime habitat. There is a village in Sicily in which the name Serio is quite common. The territory of southern Italy and Sicily was occupied in ancient times by the Greeks and then by the Romans. After the fall of the Roman Empire when the northern half of Italy was controlled by the Pope and various European princes, the southern half remained in Byzantine hands until it was eventually seized in turn by Saracens, Franks, Catalans, and many others. Southern Italians might have various strains of Greek, Arab, and Spanish in their bloodlines.

There is some irony in that after Anna (one of the daughters of Luigi) married a Lebanese Maronite named Abood, Anna's brothers and sisters teased her children about their Arab ancestry. Most likely there is Byzantine and Arab blood in the Serio line. On the European continent there probably isn't any such thing as a pure race. Adolf Hitler's search for the true Aryan was as elusive as any mythic quest. Almost any family that seeks to discover its own origins will find that its ancestry is mixed. Even the Queen of England is descended from several strains. This is what makes life interesting, diverse, healthy, and human.

Every family has its own story to tell. Families teach us that we are connected, not only to each other, but also to our past, to our roots, to the continuing process that brought us to this time and place and that will continue until physical life ceases on this planet.

Occasionally someone would tell me that he had planned to read the Bible from cover to cover, probably more for penance than insight. But when he came to the "begats," he found that to be a roadblock around which he felt compelled to make a detour. Who cares whether Joktan was the father of Hazarmaveth? Who were they and why should they be important? The genealogies were nothing more than resources for the strange and obscure names with which the sects would afflict their children.

And yet the genealogies are important—as important as the West African *griot*, the keeper of the oral tradition who runs his fingers down the memory board or knotted cord reciting the stories of his tribe. To remember the stories and traditions of your family is to provide a bond that unites us not only to our brothers, sisters, cousins, and other contemporary

# FAMILIA

relatives, but also to the long line of our forebears stretching back as far as recorded history and memory permit.

In this day of the "Great Disconnect," when the world is expanding exponentially, moving us away from one another, it is so important to remember our stories and pass them on to our children.

# TABLE OF MEMORIES

MARIA GRACIA HAD LUPUS for many years and was now dying of cancer. She was the last of the family to live in my grandfather Luigi's house on Garrison Street in Newark's Ironbound section. It seems that as one approaches death, the memories of the past take on a particular poignancy to the extent that even incidental experiences are magnified to life-changing turning points. We talked about those memories. I remembered the words of Joy Ufema, a thanatologist who once said that when you are on your death bed the only thing that you will have left will be your memories, so make sure they are good ones. And we did have good memories to share.

Mary, as she was called, was one of ten children. My grandfather was married twice. When his first wife died, he married her sister, so my aunts and uncles were not only brothers and sisters, or half-brothers and half-sisters, but also cousins. But more important, they were family.

I remember as a child the large kitchen table around which the family would gather for Sunday dinner. It was the same table they would use to work on artistic projects, and later at night to play games and share stories. It was to this table that they brought their boyfriends and girlfriends, and later their husbands and wives, and then the grandchildren. The table was the center of our family's life. It had the color of soft caramel and the peppermint-green design stamped into its metal top is still impressed on my memory.

Before I left the basement kitchen, I asked Mary whatever became of that table. She said that it was in the back part of the cellar. I looked in and there it was, covered with paint cans and tools and seldom used housewares. And yet, in its state of dereliction I could still hear the sound of laughter and love and taste the bread and wine of distant memory that still holds us together.

All our family gatherings were celebrated with huge amounts of food. My Italian grandmother would call us to the table with *"manga, manga,"* and my German grandmother would bid us *"essen,"* though sometimes she would say to the kids, *"fressen"*—the word used when cattle feed. Brothers and sisters, aunts and uncles, and all the cousins who had not seen one another for long periods of time would sit down and talk. Even those who had disagreements with other members of the family would put aside their differences and actually acknowledge each other's presence and, at the very least, make small talk. Breaking bread together is able to do something for the bonding of people that nothing else can do. The hunger of the stomach is mild compared to the gnawing hunger of the heart. Gandhi was right when he said that to one who is starving, God often appears in the form of bread.

When Jesus told Peter to feed his sheep, he was talking about the spiritual needs of his flock—spiritual needs that are part of the human hunger. We may not live by bread alone, but there is a strong connection between the spiritual and the physical. If you are starving, you are not interested in philosophy. This is why the church has a mandate to be concerned about those who are in need. You cannot separate the physical from the spiritual.

For Luke, table companionship, eating a meal with others, opens people's lives to the presence of the risen Christ. Some scholars argue about whether or not the meal that Jesus shared with the two disciples on the Emmaus Road was the sacrament of Holy Communion. That's not the point! What Luke is trying to tell us is that whenever or wherever we share a meal with others, there is a sacramental aspect to the meal because Christ is present.

Christ was present at our family table, but never mentioned or acknowledged, except for the occasional, "Oh, for Christ's sake!" which never had any religious significance. The divine presence was in the relationships.

My most frequent recollection of the Serio family is that they were a fun-loving group, always joking with one another. I can't recall too many serious conversations—even the deaths, whether natural or otherwise, of acquaintances had some dark humor in it, as though laughter would dispel the inner terror like whistling in the cemetery at night. At the funeral of family members, in the midst of sadness there was always some amusement. When my uncle Gene died and was "laid out" at the Buyus Funeral

# THE DWELLING PLACE OF WONDER

Home, the first night of the wake we commented on how appropriate it was that he had a smile on his lips, as though the joke was on us. Gene had finished his course and now was enjoying our struggles through life. By the next night the undertaker had removed the smile.

Gene epitomized the mood of the fifties. I remember him in his khaki slacks, his love for opera and Broadway, and his curiosity and willingness to try new things. He always seemed to have some art or craft project going on. On a trip to Las Vegas he brought back for me a box of rock samples from the desert. It is one of the few gifts from childhood that I still possess. When he died, my grandmother gave me the ciborium that was used at his funeral mass. I still use it each year as a chalice at Christmas Eve candlelight communion.

The Serios knew how to entertain themselves, usually at each other's expense. When tape recorders first became available for home use, the Serios had one—it was probably Gene's. He would conduct "Man-in-the-Street" interviews after the format of some radio personality named "Mr. Anthony." On one occasion Gene lowered the microphone through the heating grate above the kitchen stove (houses were usually heated by a stove in the basement, the heat rising through a grate to warm the room above). Luigi was yelling at his wife, Angelina—he did this often, and she always ignored him—and he was recorded on tape. When it was played back, he was so angry that he stormed upstairs yelling even louder. All of us, even Angelina, could hardly keep from laughing.

Luigi had been a railroad man in the old country. His routine was precise. On a work night at exactly 9:00 p.m. he would take his wind-up alarm clock from the top of the stove and climb the steps to his bedroom. From then on it was expected that the noise and chatter would diminish. It seldom did. My sister-in-law, Carole, learned the house rules one particular night when the table fellowship was especially raucous. As soon as they heard Luigi's footsteps on the stairs, all the children scattered out the door or to the back room, except for Carole who was left to bear the full force of Luigi's wrath. "What's a matter?" he growled, "You no gotta home?"

The Serio house on Garrison Street was small, but each person had his or her own space, and one could move from room to room, or even a part of it, and sense that person's occupation of the space. That so many children could live in three rooms always amazed me.

In late afternoons when the shadows would lengthen and the sunlight would enter the darkening room at an oblique angle and the muted sound

# TABLE OF MEMORIES

of an Italian opera could be heard in the distance, there was a feeling that we were living in another time and another place, both mysterious and secure.

Angelina was very religious. Only her daughter, Sue, seemed to inherit her piety; the rest of this second generation family had been secularized by the American culture. There was a picture of Jesus on her wall that frightened me as a young boy. The Jesus with the exposed, flaming heart was too graphic; I just didn't understand the symbolism at that age. Now in a time of open-heart surgery and antacids for heart-burn, the picture might be appropriate for some graphic advertisement. Angelina was always laughing, especially when Luigi would get angry. They fed off each other—the more she laughed, the angrier he became, until he left in disgust.

Seldom could I understand my grandmother. She never mastered the English language, and I never became fluent in Italian, but her love transcended speech. Every encounter was an opportunity for her to give you something, whether it was a coin, a piece of fruit, or some token that represented her generous spirit. Most often she wanted you to eat.

Angelina was a terrible cook. If she didn't like the taste of her pasta sauce, she would grab the nearest bottle of wine, or pour schnapps into the vegetables, or add some other ingredient that would drastically alter the taste from what one would expect. Whatever there was in the refrigerator that she wanted to get rid of ended up in the sauce. Her daughters took to preparing dinner as an act of self-defense.

But it was never the food; it was how it was prepared and served—with love. Her table was always a welcoming place. Her table would forever be a place of memory.

The Lord's table is a table of memory and of love and acceptance. We are drawn to that spiritual table because it is prepared for us and we are welcome there. All our hurts and sorrows are healed and we become whole.

In Robert Benton's story, *Places in the Heart*, the cinematic version concludes with a communion service in a small Baptist church in rural Texas. Gathered before Christ's table are friends and enemies, murderer and victim, black and white—life's protagonists and antagonists all sharing the bread and cup and offering the possibility for spiritual unity in a time to come.

When the Spirit of Christ is present, every table is holy.

# THE FARMER FROM SARATOV

Though he was born in Russia, my mother's father, Lucas Wertz, was thoroughly German, a descendant of Catherine the Great's peasant migration of 1763. His ancestors had come from southern Germany, brought by the empress from Anhalt who had hoped the industrious Germans would serve as an example to the indolent Russians that she ruled. Later tsars would relegate these so-called Volga-Germans to serf-like status, binding them to the Russian heartland to grow wheat on the great plains. The communists would nearly exterminate them.

Lucas possessed those Germanic qualities that have distinguished that noble race since the time when they had fought with Caesar in the forests of Gaul. He had a fierce pride in who he was. A tall, handsome man whose face and clear-framed glasses reminded people of Harry Truman, he enjoyed the acknowledged resemblance and took pride in this small link to American greatness. He had pursued the American dream and was content with its fulfillment.

I never heard the story of how he came to America. Perhaps he felt the early rumblings of revolution in Imperial Russia or saw liberty's faint glow on another shore. I wish I could have asked him why he left, what stars he saw, what voices he heard; what consuming passion drives a man to leave one world for another? Perhaps the myth is better than the reality, and a fragment of memory more comforting than truth.

This farmer from Saratov came to Newark, New Jersey, not far from the gates of the new world at Ellis Island. He was content with a small framed house on a tree-shaded street in a German-speaking neighborhood, a family of three daughters, a son who served his country in the Navy and then struck gold in the postwar California real-estate market, and a good wife, also from Russia, who always had his dinner served at the required hour. His social life centered around his church where he served in the honored position as Elder and as president of the church's Board of Trustees. He also had other gifts that were seldom spoken of.

The Pennsylvania Germans, who are of the same ethnic stock, believed that their *braucherei*, also known as "pow-wow doctors," had, in addition to their gifts of healing, certain psychic abilities, especially precognition. The lore of the braucher, with its many spells and incantations, could be passed from one generation to the next, only by alternating gender. Thus, a father could teach a daughter, but not a son, to practice the braucher's art. There also seems to be a transmission of certain arcane gifts that were acquired not through any verbal or observable methods, but simply by being in the presence of the person.

Perhaps one day it might be discovered that all our knowledge, personality, behavioral patterns—all that makes each of us truly unique—is not merely a formation of the brain, but resides in the spirit of the person. There is a mind beyond the brain. There is a way of knowing that goes beyond the empirical method, a *"tertium organum"* as Peter Ouspensky, the Russian esotericist, described it.

When you have established a strong relationship with someone, you begin to pick up clues that let you know what he is thinking or feeling. Some of this may be attributed to the art of discerning nearly imperceptible signs in body language, tone, or feelings, based on previous experience. Much might be explained by conventional behavioral science.

However, there are events in our lives when we seem to "know" something without the benefit of our senses—the extrasensory perception. Human history is replete with accounts of precognition, from Caesar's dreams to the many psychic accounts surrounding the sinking of the Titanic to the tragedy of September 11, 2001, although in many cases the predictions were made after the fact.

Lucas Wertz never admitted to having psychic abilities. I doubt if he even knew the meaning of the word. However, there were several incidents that now cause me to believe that he had this sixth sense, and that some of his abilities were transmitted to his daughter, my mother.

We were living in a third-floor apartment on Monroe Street. Lucas loved to walk—a few miles was nothing to him compared to the great distances he must have walked in the region around Saratov. He often walked the mile or so to our place on a Saturday afternoon.

## THE DWELLING PLACE OF WONDER

On this particular Saturday he arrived late. He was baby-sitting while my mother went out for the evening. My brother and I had already been put to bed, but we were not yet asleep. I had a double bed to myself and my two-year-old brother, George, was in his crib in the corner. Mom was in the kitchen putting on her finishing touches. Lucas was having a cup of coffee.

In the middle of their conversation, with no explanation whatsoever, Lucas stood up and calmly walked into the bedroom, picked up George from the crib and carried him into the kitchen. No sooner had they left the room there was a crack and a loud crashing thud. The bedroom was suddenly filled with plaster dust. I was covered in gypsum flakes and white powder and emerged from the covers coughing through the dust.

Mom and Lucas rushed into the room and brought me out before any more damage ensued. They saw that the plaster in the ceiling had come loose and fell in the corner of the room over George's crib. Had not Lucas picked him up, he would have been crushed. Covered in dust by the side of the bed was my Little Golden Book and its story of Chicken Little.

Lucas seemed to know things that struck me as unusual, though he never talked about his own personal faith. There was always a special connection between us. During his last illness as he lay dying of stomach cancer, he was appreciative of my visits, but embarrassed by his loss of dignity. Our conversations were superficial, but behind the words was a strong bond. The night Lucas died, I had been working on a project at the Boy's Club. I was using a band saw to cut a piece of wood, being extremely careful with this tool. In the midst of my concentration I felt as if someone was standing alongside of me, and a chill came over me. It was enough of a distraction to cause me to nick my finger with the blade of the saw. The sight of the sudden loss of blood was enough to bring on an ebbing of consciousness through which Lucas' presence became very strong. After my wound was bound, I walked the long mile home anxious for my mother's healing words and some rest.

The apartment was empty. Rose came up from her first floor apartment and told me that Lucas had died and that Mom had gone to Marne Street. I sat at the kitchen table and waited, staring in silence at the spot where Lucas often had his cup of coffee. A few hours later, Mom came home and told me that her father had died. It was precisely the time I had felt his presence at the Boy's Club. To this day, whenever I look at the scar on my ring finger, I remember Lucas and wish that he had chosen a better time to make his final appearance.

## THE FARMER FROM SARATOV

Lucas' wisdom was more mechanical than it was intellectual. When Uncle Richie returned from the Navy, he and Lucas decided to go into the tool and die business. They constructed a small three-room factory in the backyard. It seemed that everything in the city was done in miniature. There just wasn't enough room. But the tool and die shop appeared big at the time, and I helped build it, though I was only seven years old.

In those days, with memories of the Great Depression less than a decade old, one made do with what one had or could obtain for free. Richie kept his eye open for used building materials. When an old factory was torn down in another part of the city, he and Lucas and I got into his old Ford pickup and went for the bricks. The shop went up in one summer.

Dreams do not die; they evolve into something else. In a few years the shop was closed and Richie was humming "California, Here I Come." He had found his spiritual rainbow with the Jehovah's Witnesses and sought his pot of gold on the opposite coast.

There never is a pot of gold at the end of the rainbow, because rainbows are seen from one's own particular perspective. You see it when you are in a mist, and should you travel to where you think the rainbow ends, you find that there is no end, just another beginning. The treasure of the rainbow is in the beauty of its vision, its hopes, its dreams. It's good to follow one's dreams as long as they keep receding into the future and you recognize that you are continually in a state of becoming.

Richie settled in California and worked at an assortment of odd jobs. He and his wife, Barbara, held positions as butler and housekeeper for the actor James Cagney. He thought it unusual that the Cagneys saw their children only by appointment, and only at certain times of the day. What other stories they could have told. Richie was also a horticulturist, and then he began dabbling in real estate in the Los Angeles area. Those were boom times for land development and he made a fortune. He later moved to Oregon where he also continued to sell real estate before he died of a heart attack.

Richard and Barbara Wertz crossed the country several times in the fifties, but the only stories I heard were of Jehovah's Witness theology, of how blood transfusions, Christmas, and aluminum pots were bad for you. It didn't bother me about the transfusions or cooking in aluminum pots, but not celebrating Christmas was an entirely different matter. I felt sorry for their kids who seemed to proliferate in biblical proportions with every trip east. Nevertheless, I delighted in sending them a religious card every Christmas.

The trips east were not so much for family reunions as they were for the Jehovah's Witness conventions. There was a particularly big one at Yankee Stadium one year. Campgrounds were set up in New Jersey and New York where Witnesses from all over the world could pitch their tents and park their campers. In the fifties, American highways were wide open and people were on the move. I was impressed with the huge numbers of people attending the religious gathering. When you can show the world how many people you can pack into Yankee Stadium, you create the thought that if so many thousands of people believe their doctrines, there might be some truth to it. Numbers may work in politics and business, but religious truth shouldn't be determined by how many adherents it has or how many converts it makes.

When Charles Russell founded his sect in the nineteenth century, he had the revelation that only 144,000 would make it into heaven. When his group grew to a few million worldwide, some were getting short-changed. Richie couldn't persuade me to join a religion that had limited occupancy in the hereafter.

I was also bothered by their constant predictions of the end of the world, which they seemed to make with regularity every other decade. Originally known as the Millennial Dawnists, the group was founded with the expectation that the cosmic curtain would be drawn in 1874. And then it was 1914. And then 1918. And then 1925. I don't know how many times since then, but Richie was now pushing for 1975. I suppose if you keep making these predictions, you will eventually get it right. But who was going to be around to say "I told you so"?

Richie sold his home in San Diego, bought another one in Tujunga, and realized the fortune that could be made in the burgeoning real estate market. Years later, he cashed in and moved to the Rogue River area of Oregon where he was not so successful. His wealth was not compatible with his religion, however, and eventually he drifted from his church, although his family continued in the faith. Richie's faith journey has raised the question of whether a person's life experiences determine what his spiritual expression will be, or does a person's faith shape and mold his character and experience?

# THE FARMER FROM SARATOV

Of course it is both. That's why it is called a "spiritual journey." Everyone is on such a journey. We are continually in a state of becoming as faith shapes life and life speaks to faith.

I wish I had had the opportunity to discuss this with Richie, and with Lucas. I can only guess that Lucas' spirituality was traditional and deep. I was too young to have deep philosophical and theological discussions with this simple man of simple tastes and rigid ways.

Lucas lived by the clock and by the calendar. Five days a week he worked at the weaver's trade, coming home on schedule and demanding that his dinner be served exactly at 6:00 p.m. Soup was required at every meal, usually chicken. Dinner had to be eaten in silence—even a slurp was met with a stare.

After dinner, Lucas would go upstairs and take down a wooden cigar box in which he kept his tobacco and cigarette papers. He used a rolling machine by which he made his cigarettes in a very precise manner. After listening to the radio and his favorite programs, "The Lone Ranger" and "The Shadow" among them, he would retire. It was a pattern from which he seldom deviated.

Today our lives are seldom routine and are filled with overcrowded calendars and multitasking. We have lost the freedom that comes from a disciplined life that provides space for family, for simple joys and special graces, and for interior maintenance of one's soul. It is in remembering this plain farmer from Saratov that my heart longs for his wisdom that was lost because I never recognized it as such at the time, but now that I have reached his age I have come to value.

# THE MAD MONK

NATALIA GRAUBERGER STOOD WITH her monogrammed leather luggage in front of Castle Clinton at the foot of Manhattan. She had completed an arduous sea voyage that began in the Black Sea port of Sebastopol after leaving her native Czaritzyn. Across the New York Bay, many of her co-voyagers were being processed through immigration at Ellis Island, but Natalie had traveled first class, enjoyed conversation with the captain, and dined at his table. She stood alone with the bags her father had crafted for her in his leather factory, waiting to begin a new life in a new world. A proud woman, she was grateful that she did not have to undergo the often demeaning process that awaited the steerage passengers on the isle of hope and tears.

She came to America with an offer of marriage from Mr. Ellenberger, from the same Volga-German community in which she had been raised, only to learn that Mr. Ellenberger had tired of waiting and had married another. It did not take long for her to be noticed by another Volga-German, a tall, handsome farmer from Saratov who had found a new occupation as a weaver in this wonderful land of opportunity.

My grandparents, Lucas and Natalie, were descendants of industrious German farmers that Catherine the Great invited to settle in new lands that had been added to the Russian Empire. Catherine wanted to show the Russians how hard work, technological skill, and a strong sense of community could produce abundant crops in the region around the Volga River. It didn't take much to persuade these Germans to leave their homes in Anhalt, the Palatinate, Hesse, Mannheim, and Schleswig-Holstein. In the two hundred years since the Protestant Reformation, Europe had been devastated by wars. The Seven Years War of 1756–1763 was the last straw.

# THE MAD MONK

Louis XV had sent his troops into southwestern Germany to lay waste to the land and completely destroy the infrastructure. Poverty, enforced servitude in the military, heavy taxation, and religious persecution made living conditions intolerable. While many of these Palatine Germans found their way to America and joined existing communities, most notably the "Pennsylvania Dutch," some thirty thousand accepted the Empress' invitation to move eastward. The carrot at the end of the stick came in the form of large tracts of land available for purchase, freedom from taxation and military conscription, religious freedom and a measure of self-determination, and financial assistance in establishing their communities.

For more than a century these Volga-Germans endured hardships, Cossack raids, burning and pillaging, but they continued to prevail and even to flourish. By the latter part of the nineteenth century their numbers exceeded 1.7 million. Some, like Natalie's parents, actually managed to rise in the ranks of the upper middle class so that their children could receive a good education and enjoy the fruits of their labors.

However, a "Russification" process had begun under Czar Alexander in 1874, and the emigration of Volga-Germans to the American frontier had begun. The first decade of the twentieth century brought many changes. The dark clouds of unrest began to gather and the four horsemen of the apocalypse were saddling their steeds, ready to bring war, famine, pestilence, and death to Mother Russia and to the rest of Europe. Those who could see these portents and had the resources followed the earlier émigrés to America. Many who had endured the turmoil of previous periods of persecution or depression felt they could weather whatever storm might appear. They would be terribly wrong.

So in 1910 Natalie left her father and mother and her ten brothers and sisters and made the journey down the Volga to the Black Sea, the Mediterranean and across the Atlantic.

Lucas and Natalie were married and bought a house on Bremen Street in a German-speaking section of Newark, New Jersey. The two-story, four-room dwelling was one of hundreds built in the 1880s in the "Down Neck" area of the city, later to be called "the Ironbound" because it was surrounded by rail lines. The houses all looked the same, like a lineup of houses on a Monopoly board. In these four small rooms—kitchen, front parlor, and two bedrooms—Lucas and Natalie raised their son and three daughters.

# THE DWELLING PLACE OF WONDER

After the death of my grandfather in 1954 and my parents' divorce, my mother, my two brothers, and I moved into 89½ Marne Street. It was during this time that I heard the stories of life in Imperial Russia.

Natalie had a picture of the imperial family—Nicholas and Alexandra, and their children, Marie, Olga, Tatiana, Anastasia, and Alexei. She would bring it out and grieve over their deaths at Ekaterinburg. What a handsome man, she would say of Nicholas, and such beautiful children. I found myself falling in love with Grand Duchess Tatiana and wondering what it would have been like to live in St. Petersburg.

Dreams have a way of distorting reality. They often leave out the dark side, the unpleasantness that mars one's reverie. St. Petersburg native, Svetlana Boym, refers to nostalgia as a "hypochondria of the heart." It is a yearning for a time that never was, a false memory that becomes a reality of our own design because we choose not to face the truth.

Natalie had a yearning for her homeland and the family she left behind. She would not speak about the misery of the Russian peasants, virtual slaves of the aristocracy, and the horrors of their menial existence. The massacres of the Jews in the many pogroms that occurred were not part of her consciousness, nor did she speak of the great famine of 1891 that affected the area of the Volga where she lived when she was six years old.

Natalie was upper middle class, a privileged element of Russian society that would lose everything in the coming revolution. She was fluent in seven languages: German, Russian, Ukranian, Polish, Dutch, English, and Farsi. I asked her why she spoke Farsi. "We had Persian servants," she said. "We had to tell them what to do, and they would teach us their language."

Her father not only made luggage, but crafted fine footwear. He made ballet slippers for one of the tsar's daughters and leather boots for the imperial household. She recalled going with her father one day to make a delivery and encountering a strange looking man emerging from the palace. It was none other than the mad monk, Grigori Novykh, known to history as Rasputin.

Natalie said that he was frightening to behold, and she backed away so fast that she nearly stumbled. He stared at her briefly with penetrating eyes that she never forgot. It was a peculiar brush with history. Rasputin had bewitched the tzarina, who had hoped that he might affect a cure for her hemophiliac son, Alexei, but Rasputin simply used the imperial connections to influence Alexandra who ruled in Nicholas' absence while he was administering the military forces in the Great War.

# THE MAD MONK

There are those who regard Rasputin as a mystic and saint, a holy man, a *"starets"* who put aside the things of this world to concentrate on praying for the salvation of those souls who still lived here.

He was far from a devout servant of Christ. He lived a life of excess and debauchery, engaging in the wildest of carnal delights, using the rationale that salvation can only come through repentance, but before one can repent one must first sin. Even Martin Luther, whose confessor advised him to "sin boldly," knew that one "must believe and rejoice in Christ even more boldly." Rasputin bestowed his blessings upon those aristocratic noblewomen who acceded to his spiritual distortions, without offering the blessing that comes from the life of faithful devotion to Christ.

Rasputin was reputed to be a psychic, not only in his ability to heal by therapeutic touch, but he was also a seer who predicted his own death. He once said that if he should die at the hands of a Romanov, the entire dynasty would crumble within two years. When he was poisoned, shot, and drowned by Prince Felix Yussoupov, the murder of the imperial family occurred within two months.

Natalie would never forget how close she came to this personification of evil and always referred to him as the one responsible for the fall of Imperial Russia.

Evil has many disguises, but is most dangerous when it comes in the form of one who pretends to be holy. While I have known a few fallen servants of God, those who deliberately cloak themselves in the cloth of the religious to carry out their nefarious aims are the most despicable.

It seemed that Natalie's encounter with the mad monk had left a very deep impression. It also taught me to be wary of latter day "messiahs" who use religion to attain power, wealth, and influence and often misdirect it for their own personal and political gain.

# AMONG THE GLADIATORS

My father was a fighter. A lean, scrappy kid with a hair-trigger temper who moved up the ladder from street brawls to the boxing ring. Danny Ardito taught him how to control his powder-keg nature and wait for the right opportunity to ignite and direct the explosive wrath of a frustrated childhood.

When my grandfather's first wife died after bearing two children, Luigi married her sister. My father was her first-born. His older brother and sister were also cousins. Seven other siblings were to follow to comprise a family of twelve. For an immigrant from Italy this was enough to fertilize the new soil of the American dream and roots took hold.

Dad bought into that dream, but he didn't want to wait. He had to reach the pinnacle as quickly as possible and break out of the Italian ghetto. As the asphalt basketball courts in today's urban playgrounds fuel the hopes of young African-Americans, so the boxing ring became the arena of my father's dreams.

Harry Serio was regarded as a tough fighter who never backed away from an opponent. One writer said that he combined the art of boxing with his great speed and power punching. He won the Golden Gloves as a welterweight in 1940 and retired with a record of 38–5. In 1987 he was inducted into the New Jersey Boxing Hall of Fame, one of his proudest moments.

My earliest memories of travels with Dad were to the run-down gymnasiums and converted warehouses where punching bags were hung from rafters, canvas was stretched over springless mattresses, and ropes were tied to two-by-fours embedded in buckets of sand at the corners.

## AMONG THE GLADIATORS

Two-Ton Tony Galento, the heavyweight contender and the only man to knock Joe Louis down before losing the bout, made a guest appearance at the Rivoli Theater. He had a minor role in the classic Marlon Brando film, "On the Waterfront." He was waiting for a cab after the crowds had left. I had heard that he had sparred with my father, but it was more likely Tony threw a punch at him in some bar. Dad was fortunate Tony didn't connect. I asked Tony if he remembered my father.

"Yeah, kid, I remember him. Good fighter. Knows how to take a punch. How's he doing?"

Before I could answer, he got into the taxi and was off, and I was left wondering, "Could I have been a contender if I had taken seriously my father's encouragement and urging?"

My father wanted me to follow in his footsteps as a boxer, but I could never master the footwork. He thought that exposure to the gyms and boxing arenas, the smell of sweat and blood, would somehow entice me into the glamorous world of mayhem and that I would find fulfillment in inflicting pain on others. He expected me to learn the fine art of strategic assault and battery, breaking down an opponent's defenses and knocking him to the canvas before he could do the same to me. The Golden Rule of the ring was "do unto your opponent before he has a chance to do unto you."

The hardwood floors, the smell of sweat and blood, the sound of leather against leather, and sometimes bone, are vivid. By the age of seven I had seen all I wanted of open wounds and broken teeth and bruised eyes.

One Sunday afternoon at the ring, Dad put a pair of boxing gloves on my hands and said, "You've got to learn to defend yourself." He taught me to keep my left up and lead with my right, occasionally jabbing with the left. Stay on your toes and move fast: it's harder to hit a moving target. I learned the art of bobbing and weaving, of constant motion. Feints are important, and so is taking a hit in order to assess whom you are up against. These are lessons that could be applied to life as well as to the ring.

The following Christmas I found under the tree my own pair of Everlast gloves. Dad also had a punching bag mounted on a flexible metal rod. After suiting up and trying on the gloves, I went to war with the bag. I gave it a good shot, putting all of my 65 lbs. behind the jab. The bag hit back, smacking me in the face. I had had it with boxing.

Boxing is both an art and a science—the same as war. It is the art of patience and opportunity, of vigilance and attack, of discovering and exploiting the weakness of your opponent. Evander Holyfield notwithstanding, it is not a Christian sport.

There was also the matter of paying your dues. Ever since the Marquess of Queensbury imposed a set of rules, there were those who tried to bend them. Boxing was a sport that straddled the borders of respectability. Thugs in tuxedos at boxing events always seemed a bit paradoxical. There were often bits of chicanery and questionable legalities. One never knew whether a fight was legit. Young fighters on their way up were sometimes told that the only way to advance their careers was to throw an occasional fight. In that way, everybody could make some money.

Dad was asked to take a dive and he agreed. In the ring, however, his opponent hit him a little too hard in the jaw. It was enough to infuriate my father, and he fought back and won the bout.

While boxing never really appealed to me, I did try Graeco-Roman wrestling. It certainly wasn't a career move, but I learned a lot in three lessons. The instructor was a college kid working with neighborhood guys at Wilson Avenue School. He approached wrestling like Sun Tsu's *Art of War*, seeking ways to win by exploiting your opponent's weaknesses. Wrestling was more cerebral than knocking your adversary senseless.

You circled the ring and studied your opponent, testing his defenses and reflexes with your feints. You learned not to commit too soon, and did so only when you were sure. You did not want your aggressive move turned against you. When you committed to the take-down, you did so wholeheartedly. It was a zen-like action, without conscious thought. If you thought too much, you could outwit yourself. You had to trust your instincts and training and put your actions into the hands of a higher power.

An early lesson I learned from wrestling was that sometimes the best way to deal with a problem was to engage it directly rather than to try to escape from it. If your opponent has you entangled in a predicament, turn towards him, not away. Your advantage is most often gained when you seize the initiative.

In Genesis, Jacob wrestled throughout the night with an unknown stranger that turned out to be an aspect of the divine, and emerged from his ordeal scarred, but blessed. For centuries, those close to God have wrestled with angels in the dark night of the soul and been tormented, some to the point of insanity. It is because of their anguished struggles with God's presence, as well as God's absence, that we have the gifts of their encounters, not only in their words but in the majesty of their deeds.

## AMONG THE GLADIATORS

Sometimes we are broken by God and carry the wounds with us for a lifetime, like Jacob's disjointed hip, but God also heals and uses our wounds to bring healing to others.

Paul referred to shadow boxing when discussing the importance of being conditioned for warfare with the world. He does not "box as one who beats the air," but in all things exercises self-control and is deliberate in where he will land his punches.

I soon found that boxing and wrestling were not sports in which I wanted to invest my life. While there were some useful applications and valuable principles, they were additional tools in the toolbox for living. You still had to know when the hammer was more appropriate than the screwdriver. As in many sports where one individual contends against another, the object is to emerge victorious by defeating your opponent. Our competitive society glorifies the individual whose advancement is made possible by the defeat of an adversary, whether a personal rival or a corporate competitor in the marketplace.

Paul also used a metaphor about runners competing against one another for an imperishable prize. That seems inconsistent with my instinctive feelings about the mercy of God. I have always distrusted those who professed a belief in a personal salvation to the exclusion of the redemption of the world. We are not competing for top seeds in the hereafter, but rather we share the same spirit of God that is in each of us and need to strive together as members of one team so that we are all victorious in the end.

# THE SUNSHINE HOOK

THE AMERICAN DREAM FOR many immigrant families began in basements and coal cellars. Those who left the old world with nothing more than the clothes they wore and whatever possessions they could stuff into their cloth satchels and cardboard luggage wanted nothing more than to own their own home in which to raise a family, a job that paid a decent wage, and the security to know that no one, no government, was going to rob them of their dreams.

They came to the cities where they could find employment, walk to work or take public transportation, but most importantly, be surrounded by fellow landsmen who spoke the same language and continued their traditions and culture. It was a haven of familiarity in a strange land.

My grandparents, both the Serios and Wertzes, were happy finally to be able to purchase their own houses. They were small and cramped considering the number of children that they raised, and the backyards were infinitesimally small compared to the farms they had worked on in Campania and the Russian plateau. As their families grew and more space was needed, there was no room for expansion. The houses in the Ironbound section of Newark were either attached row homes or single dwellings with three- or four-foot wide alleys between them. Sometimes there was room to build out the back.

However, the least expensive method was to convert the basements into kitchens and to change from coal furnaces to oil heat in order to make usable space from the coal bins. The Wertzes had a small woodstove in the basement that heated the house through open grates in the floor. Heat was regulated by opening and closing the grates.

# THE SUNSHINE HOOK

The wood that was used were the scraps from pattern shops. They came in a variety of shapes and sizes. It was fun to build things out of these irregular wooden forms before they were consigned to the stove.

The basement kitchen was the gathering place for the family. Lucas Wertz was a stern and regimented Volga-German who insisted that meals be punctual and eaten in silence. But once dinner was over and Lucas ascended the stairs to roll his cigarette and listen to his radio program, the children were free to talk and to discuss the day's events. In the Serio basement they often had to devise their own entertainments and amusements, from art to interactive games. Bingo, poker and other card games, and board games were brought out after the evening meal. It was a place to bring boyfriends and girlfriends. A place to be family.

During the day the kitchen was a place of muted light and shadow. Light from the outside came through the small basement windows that were hooked open to allow the sun and air to penetrate. Natalie Wertz, who would spend her life in this room and bring comfort to her children and her grandchildren, instructed me in the art of transcendence and the mysticism of ordinary experience.

There were times when I would bear the cuts and bruises of daily play and come crying to her healing arms. She would hold me close and point to the sunshine hook, a simple twist of metal that held open the cellar window and allowed a shaft of pure white light to illuminate the minute particles in the air. She meant only to distract, to divert my attention from the wounds and scratches of a child's warfare with the world, but I was fascinated by the interplay of light and shadow and the reflection from the specks of dust that were everywhere around us, but which could only be seen in the light.

It was as if the world had changed, but it was only because I was now looking at it from a different perspective, in a new light. Suddenly I became aware of a new way of seeing. The intricacies of the dandelion in the backyard became an object of wonder. I thought of all the things that existed in the world and how they were made up of an infinite number of parts. How do we direct our consciousness to comprehend it all? We see the multiplicity of Creation, but it is we who impose our meaning on what we see. It is for poets and mystics to see beyond seeing and to help us to become aware of what is present in our everyday lives but overlooked by our own priorities of living. Our world is filled with wonder and mystery if only we had the mindfulness to be aware.

## THE DWELLING PLACE OF WONDER

My second-floor bedroom was not heated except for the bit of warmth that ascended through the stairwell. On a cold January night, after my grandmother would tuck me in under the heavy blankets, I would lie awake and watch the moonlight through the frosted windows and think of other worlds and how vast must be the mind of God to conceive of so much. Years later, after seeing the movie *Dr. Zhivago*, the image that held particular poignancy was that of young Yuri, on the night of his mother's burial, lying in bed listening to the rapping of a branch against the window as the sound of the balalaika added another layer to the growing complexity of experiencing life.

It is the frame of reference that transforms the ordinary into moments of ecstasy or despair. Meursault, in Albert Camus's *The Stranger*, observes everything at his mother's funeral: "the bright new screws in the walnut-stained coffin, the colors of the nurse's clothes, the large stomachs of the old ladies who had been his mother's closest friends, the whiteness of the roots in her grave." The existentialist finds meaning in the moment, but those who see in the moment the totality of life soar to much larger worlds.

I went to grade school in the days when desks were bolted to the floor and arranged in rows, indicative of the rigid system of education practiced at that time in which learning was a body of knowledge funneled into a receptive brain. You were graded on how much you could absorb and regurgitate on an exam paper. Winston Churchill once remarked that his education was only interrupted by his schooling. We learn not only by the accumulation of facts, but by the integration and interpretation of life experiences.

Childhood is the dwelling place of wonder and imagination. Too soon we pass from it. There needs to be a place for fantasy, astonishment, and the sheer joy of discovery of that which you don't understand, but which would be made clear either by science or personal revelation.

I watched a ladybug crawl on the back of Diane Podres's neck in Miss Gless's fifth grade class. The slow movement of its polka-dot shell contrasted with the twitching of her neck and the movement of her bright golden hair. I stared at the bug as it made its way through the folds and patterns of her green dress to the nape of her neck, wondering if and when she would feel the light pressure of tiny bug feet on her skin and whether I should swat it into oblivion. I still wonder about the significance of that particular bug. It has served its purpose in the fragment of memory that has endured over the years.

## THE SUNSHINE HOOK

The sunshine hook, for those brief moments, suspended my fears and held back the tears, and brightened all the mornings that were to come. I could look forward in hope, realizing that this moment in time was simply one experience of so many more that would comprise my future.

# THE ROLLING GARDENS OF PACIFIC STREET

UNCLE NICK WAS THE family patriarch, a title achieved mostly through longevity, although his wisdom was nothing to be trifled with. One would never know it to look at him, but within the family he was reputed to be fabulously wealthy—a fact he carefully concealed from everyone, including his only son, Louis, the banker, and his wife, Flo, who labored in a sweatshop well into her seventies when failing eyesight forced her retirement.

Nick possessed only one suit, a narrow-lapelled black worsted purchased back in the sixties to wear at the funeral of his brother, and subsequently at family funerals since. He bought a new suit that he wore to his older sister's funeral some twenty years later, perhaps because he had become the titular head of the family.

"One man's trash is another man's fortune," so they say. Nick made his fortune during the war collecting scrap metal and parlaying it into a sizeable sum. It was during this time that his ingenuity became legendary.

Rubber was a very scarce commodity. In order to make a buck, Nick removed the rubber hoses from his old Ford's cooling system and replaced it with an intricate network of pipes and connectors. It worked beautifully. That is, until one day that a friend borrowed the car and it overheated on McCarter Highway, just outside of Newark. They pushed it to a nearby garage and lifted the hood. The attendant took one look at the pipes, which gave the appearance of a distillery on wheels and said, "You don't need a mechanic. You need a plumber!"

When it came to auto improvisation, Nick was a genius. There was a time back in the thirties when Nick drove an old truck from Scranton,

# THE ROLLING GARDENS OF PACIFIC STREET

Pennsylvania to Newark, New Jersey. The tires were badly worn and the back roads were rut-filled. When the right front tire blew, Nick put on the spare. Then the left rear tire went. Fortunately he had an extra inner tube and he changed the tube and pumped it up. But when twenty-four miles from his destination, both front tires went, there was little to do.

Relying on his experience and expertise, Nick packed both tires with dirt and continued his journey with a less-than-comfortable ride.

My brother Bob, Uncle Emilio, and I visited Nick at his Pacific Street estate in the Ironbound section of Newark. It was a modest property. Bars and barbed wire protected the back yard. A "Beware of Dog" sign hung on the gate, warning of a junkyard dog no longer present. Flo was hanging out her laundry on the line. With all his money, we wondered why they didn't have an electric dryer, or if Flo had to do all her wash by hand. Nevertheless, Nick was concerned about providing Flo with whatever convenience he could contrive. She was standing atop some moveable stairs that Nick had rescued from the junkyard. It had been used by Eastern Airlines for boarding the old two-prop planes years ago. We marveled at the application.

"Hey, that's nothing," he said. "Let me show you my garden." There was nothing in the backyard except concrete and a four-car garage. He pushed open the doors of the garage and wheeled out his portable garden—sixteen barrels cut in half and mounted on roller skates. There were tomatoes and egg plants, a small fig tree, gladiolus, and other vegetables and flowers. "These kids around here, they'll steal anything," explained Nick. "That's why I have to lock up my garden at night."

After he watered his plants and positioned them where they would get the most sun, we sat on his swing for some lemonade and conversation. In spite of his gravelly voice and uneducated speech, Nick possessed a quick wit that could duel with any of the Serios. While he was born on a farm in southern Italy, the blood of the Italian Renaissance flowed in his veins.

It has been said that while the Swiss had lived for centuries in peace in their Alpine villages, all they could produce were cuckoo clocks. But the Italians who lived in the path of marauding armies and encountered violence at every turn gave us some of the world's finest art, the greatest operas, and a system of laws and government that have become the foundation of the world's great democracies.

Adversity is still our greatest teacher, ingrained in the fabric of our evolutionary nature. We adapt or perish. But sometimes, I wonder—to come four thousand years from the hanging gardens of Babylon to the rolling gardens of Pacific Street—whether or not it is worth it.

Still, Nick's ingenuity and ability to take what was given to him and transform it into a functional accessory serves as an example of how the human species has endured.

# RENAISSANCE MAN

ONE OF THE FAMILY associates, a Serio "wanna-be," once made the remark that when brains were being handed out to the Serio clan, Emilio was first in line and got the lion's share. I'm sure his brothers and sisters would dispute that. What they couldn't argue, however, was that he was endowed with artistic gifts that he had the intelligence to develop.

When Edward Gibbon presented his voluminous work, *The Decline and Fall of the Roman Empire*, the Duke of Gloucester was said to have remarked, "Another damned thick, heavy book! Scribble, scribble, scribble! Eh, Mr. Gibbon?"

In his preschool years, Emilio did a lot of scribbling—sidewalks, walls, notebooks, library books, toilet paper, paper napkins, restaurant tablecloths. When he ran out of writing surfaces he would draw on the back of his hands. His friends suggested that he might have a great career as a tattoo artist. But his teachers thought otherwise; they gave him paper and encouraged his artistic inclinations.

Emilio graduated in 1948 as valedictorian from Newark's Arts High School, the same school that produced the great Sarah Vaughan. He spent another year at the Newark School of Fine and Industrial Arts, which qualified him for a position as a window decorator. He decided that he didn't want to work with dummies, but the army thought otherwise, and he was drafted, trained as a medic, and put to work in Vassincourt, France. To put an artist in France is like letting a kid loose in a candy store. Emilio visited every art gallery, museum, cathedral he could get to—even the bookstalls and postcard sellers on the banks of the Seine.

Fortunately, his officers recognized his artistic abilities and put him to doing work more in keeping with his training. He was assigned to painting mess halls, decorating windows, making signs, and painting portraits. He stopped short of doing ice sculptures for the officers' mess, but may have decorated a cake or two.

The military provided Emilio access to Europe and he took advantage of it. He managed to visit our relatives in Italy and establish contacts there that were to prove very advantageous in years to come. In Italy, he studied the masters, copied their techniques, and took many photographs. He would then return to the United States where he would work as a commercial artist until he could replenish his financial resources to enable him to return to the studio that he maintained in Florence.

After his stint with the army, Emilio continued his education in the arts, studying at the Art Students League and the National Academy School of Fine Arts. He won the coveted William Aylward Award for illustration, and in the process gained the attention of Willard Cummings, who offered him a scholarship at the Skowhegan School.

Under the guidance of Cummings, who became Emilio's friend and mentor, Emilio refashioned his artistic skills from those of a commercial and graphic artist to those of a sensitive realist painter. He developed a friendship with Ben Shahn, with whom he shared some points of style, and continued his relationship with Ben's widow, Bernarda, after Ben passed away.

The Skowhegan School and his relationship with Willard Cummings were decisive milestones in Emilio's career. His work became generally known and was acquired for important private collections such as those of Vincent Price, Joseph H. Hirschhorn, Nathaniel Saltonstall, and John Eastman Jr., as well as Cummings himself. It was through Will Cummings that Emilio became friends with Bette Davis and was mentioned in her will. (Well, actually it was his paintings that were a part of her collection, which she may have bequeathed to her friend, Robin.)

As impressive as this might be, it didn't quite pay the rent. It was still a struggle. I visited Emilio in his East 80th Street apartment in Manhattan, a short walk from the Metropolitan Museum of Art, my preferred hangout during my teen years. His flat was like a set for a sitcom. As we sat in his living room overlooking the brownstone across the street where television comedian Soupy Sales was in residence, assorted characters would drop in and just as suddenly disappear. A couple came in and joined us. It was apparent that they were engaged in an identity crisis and were having trouble making the transition from beatniks to hippies. We talked about the conflicting subcultures in Manhattan and the need for maintaining one's artistic integrity while trying to survive.

Ever the gracious host, Emilio was pouring the coffee and tea and asked me to see if there were any biscuits or crackers in the refrigerator. When I opened the door to the fridge, I noticed that it was almost completely bare, except for a plate on the second shelf. Neatly arranged on the plate was a blue nightingale, feathers and all. I brought it into the living room and set it down on the coffee table as I watched my friends recoil. I asked if this was the last meal of a starving artist. Emilio said that it was just a bird that flew into his window and that he was planning on using it as a model. We didn't know whether to believe him or not. But now I always ask what he is serving for dinner.

Emilio returned to Newark in 1970 when he purchased a run-down Polish National Catholic church on Houston Street, just one block from where he grew up. Always a deeply spiritual person, Emilio nevertheless would never enter a church except for weddings, funerals, or to study an artistic work. Now he could answer his critics, "I don't have to go to church; I live in one."

Before the church could be made habitable, it first had to be exorcized—not just of demonic spirits, but thousands of pigeons. The pigeons left; some of the spirits remain. It took Emilio almost two years to convert the structure from a place of divine habitation to one more appropriate for human dwelling. He constructed a huge iconostasis or screen to segment the nave into a living room and work area. French doors were installed in the apse and the elevated altar area became the place where new idols would be created on canvas. The narthex was transformed into a gallery and reception area. The west transept became the dining room and the east transept the bedroom. Appropriately, the sacristy became purgatory—the bathroom and laundry.

At first Emilio thought about using the confessional as a telephone booth, but passed up the irony and converted it to an enclosed projection screen. Various other ecclesiastical appurtenances intermingle with antiques, memorabilia, and works of art to present a museum-like quality to the residence. Indeed, Emilio's church is on the list of many tours organized by the Brandeis University National Woman's Committee, the Newark Museum, the Unitarian Church of Montclair, the Essex County Division of Cultural Affairs, and the Preservation and Landmarks Committee, among others. Emilio welcomes the tours, especially since they provide him with the incentive to clean up his studio.

More than anything else, Emilio has been the glue that has held the Serio family together. He offers his home as a bed and breakfast for itinerant out-of-town family members, hosts the annual Christmas and New Year's Eve festivities, and with the help of nephew Danny's catering skills, supplies the reception hall for family observances. He is the communication nexus for family gossip and the listening ear to mitigate problems. He most likely spends more on coffee than he does on food. There is a tile next to his door that says *"Bienvenire casa mia! Qui fate, fate presto e andate!"* (Welcome to my house. Whatever you do, do quickly, and then go). Don't believe it. You are not only welcome in his home, but his quiet and warm personality asks you to stay.

# AUNT BETTE

EMILIO MET BETTE DAVIS in 1965 through Willard Cummings, director of the Skowhegan School of Painting and Sculpture in Maine. When a masquerade party was held at the Cheetah nightclub in Manhattan, Bette was the judge. Emilio showed up as "Mosaic Man," a pastiche of colored squares arranged like some floor in a Byzantine church. Bette loved the costume. It was the beginning of a very long friendship. Years later, when Bette's friend Robin Brown bought a cottage in East Madison, not far from Skowhegan, Bette would become a frequent visitor. With Emilio making regular trips to Skowhegan to paint and study, it was understandable that they would renew their acquaintance.

In June, 1975, Bette was invited to receive an honorary doctorate at Colby College in Waterville, Maine. Bill Cummings had become gravely ill with cancer earlier that year, and while he had invited Bette to stay at his place, he could not play host. In fact, he had been taken to the hospital and died shortly thereafter. Bette called Emilio to drive her and Robin to Maine for the funeral. It was the beginning of Emilio's career as "chauffeur to the stars."

Their trip to Maine was uneventful, and that is what made it somewhat memorable. They would stop at a picnic grounds and the Queen of Hollywood would take out a basket and prepare sandwiches, totally unrecognized by other travelers. They would stop at a hamburger joint and she would be unnoticed. It seemed to prove what hypnotists have always maintained—that you generally see what your mind prepares you to see.

Stopping for gas at an Esso station, Bette pulled out her credit card and handed it to the young boy who pumped the gas. Either he pretended not to notice the name on the card, or he may not have known who Bette was, but he did come back and tell her that her card was invalid. Emilio paid the bill as Bette muttered, "He knew who I was." They say stardom is attained when you move from being concerned that people will not recognize you to fear that they will.

Bette was appreciative of Emilio's driving ability. "I know it's not easy driving Bette Davis," she told him, "but you're one of the best drivers I've had." Emilio is a careful and considerate driver who seldom goes over the speed limit. His attitude is almost Zen-like: "where I am is where I need to be, and where I'm going will be there when I arrive."

Once, at a party at Robin's house, Bette's chauffeur arrived and Robin's husband handed him a beer. He didn't have time to put the bottle to his lips when Bette saw him and said, "No one who drinks will be driving Bette Davis! You are dismissed for the evening. Emilio will take me home!" As they left, Robin warned, "Emilio, don't stay too long." Emilio may have wondered what Robin thought he had in mind.

Bette may have been only teasing, but there may have been a yearning for what might have been. She sang a song to Emilio from *Stage Door Canteen*, "They're Either Too Young or Too Old," and she actually proposed to him. "Emilio," she said, "let's announce our engagement. That'll really shake them up." (She was fifty-six at the time; Emilio was thirty-four.)

The implications of that possibility were staggering. Aunt Bette among the Serios. She would certainly be able to hold her own with my brother Bobby and Emilio when they played movie trivia, since Bette's films were often the subject. And she could go head-to-head with John in withering put-downs. She would be amused at Tillie's malaprops, but would probably meet her match in Alma when it came to choosing the right word for a put-down. At any rate, she would never be at home in Newark, New Jersey.

Bette knew that there would never be a man strong enough for her. He would always remain in the background. Bette was very much aware of who she was, and she got to the point where John Button, the artist, observed she was doing caricatures of herself.

Commencement weekend at Colby College brought some of the cognoscenti and lesser glitterati to town and Bette suggested that they have a dinner party. She meant, of course, that Emilio would have to do all the cooking. Bette did have some domestic qualities about her; when Emilio lost a button on his brown corduroy jacket, Bette sewed it back on—with blue thread.

# AUNT BETTE

The party was well-attended. Louise Nevelson, the acclaimed American painter, was a guest, along with Jack Eastman, the director of Skowhegan, and other notables. Bette and Emilio were in the kitchen preparing some of the dishes. Emilio was looking for a platter to serve the hors d'oeuvres when Bette suggested that he serve it from his hands. Emilio passed among the guests with palms outstretched, hors d'oeuvres in one hand and nuts in the other. They didn't know what to say, but just helped themselves. Emilio returned to the kitchen and told Bette, "I had them eating out the palm of my hands." They both had a good laugh.

Unfortunately Bette's good humor was not to last very long that night. The wife of a gallery owner was entertaining the other guests with lines from Bette's movies. Bette had had enough. She stood up and glared at the woman. "I am sick and tired of your cheap imitations," she said in the best imitation of Bette Davis that evening. The poor woman was devastated and reduced to tears. She and her husband left shortly thereafter.

Louise Nevelson was next. Both she and Bette were to receive honorary doctorates the next day, but Louise treated it rather lightly. "Oh, it's just another award," she commented. Bette, who maintained a separate room for her honors, looked at her and said, "I am proud of every award I ever received. They are all important to me, and for you to say that cheapens the occasion." She stood up and stormed out of the room. Louise Nevelson then left the party, and the other guests slowly filtered out of the icy atmosphere.

Bette came downstairs a little later and observed, "Oh, they left. Hah! I guess I told them." Robin's only comment was, "What a night!"

Emilio drove Bette back to Connecticut with a brief stop at Pickens Cove where she once worked as a waitress. She invited Emilio to remain for dinner, promising him pheasant under glass. She prepared the entire meal herself, but couldn't fool Emilio—it was Cornish hen.

Dorian Harewood was a guest of Bette's when she asked Emilio to drive the actor back to Carnegie Hall. Harewood gave Emilio pointers on how to speak, and Emilio taught him how to see. There is an art to both.

When Bette admired Emilio's beautiful singing voice, Robin remarked, "No wonder. She can't sing either." But Bette was sincere in her admiration of Emilio's talent. In her autograph of the book *Mother Goddam,* she wrote: "Oh Emilio. What a cook! What an artist! Love, Bette."

Toward the end of her life when the hospitalizations became more frequent, Emilio drove up to see her. He was sitting in her room when she decided to change her gown. Robin asked Emilio to step out. Bette said to her, "Oh, it's only Emilio." I doubt that there are many men that can say they saw Bette Davis disrobe. On the other hand . . .

The telephone exchanges also were frequent. The first time Bette called, she said, "Emilio, this is Bette." "Bette who?" "Bette Davis, of course."

Another time Bette asked Robin to make the call. Robin asked, "Emilio, what are you doing?"

"Painting and watching *Mr. Skeffington*."

"Well, Mrs. Skeffington wishes to speak with you."

Robin, Bette, and Emilio were close enough that Bette often referred to the other two as her "two musketeers." It always surprised me that, as close as they were, Emilio was never mentioned in any biography of Bette, and he prefers it that way. Robin once asked him, "Emilio, you know a lot more about Bette than most people. When are you going to write a book?"

Emilio will not write a book about Bette Davis. The times they shared were personal, and he prefers that they remain so. He told me only a few of the stories of his times with Bette; the rest we can only imagine.

We live with illusion. Bette Davis was good at her craft, working in an industry that provided the necessary fantasy by which we escape our own lives in order to live some other. I suppose that is why so many fans of the stars want to know all the details of their private lives so as to become intimate with them. While I might speculate on what it would have been like to have Bette Davis as an aunt, I have my own realities to face. And they are enough.

# BILLY

BILLY MACK HAD TO be one of the most disgusting third graders in the history of Wilson Avenue School. One could understand his poverty that forced him to wear the same polo shirt for weeks on end, or the newspaper-lined shoes that his grandmother prepared for him each day to keep the rain and snow from seeping in through the holes.

Billy's mother was dead and his father was an alcoholic. I met Mr. Mack once—he gave me a dime to carry his empty wine bottles down to the trash. Billy did not see his father much. His mother, Billy's grandmother, raised Billy as best she could, but she, too, loved her whiskey. Billy was always dirty, poorly dressed, and had the most obnoxious personal habits one could imagine. He would sit at his desk and pick his nose and then lick his fingers. When Patricia, who sat across the aisle, told him to stop, he reached way back into his nostrils and offered her the biggest booger he could find.

I liked Billy for other reasons. He was a scrappy fighter and he liked me. No one picked a fight with me in the schoolyard when Billy was around. And there were always lots of fights among third graders. In those days before the schoolyard was macadamized, we spent the minutes before the last bell shooting marbles. The game was simple. You started by digging your heel into the dirt and gouging out a pocket, and then it was just like billiards. You used your marble to knock the other's guy's marble into the hole without getting in yourself. If you managed to accomplish this, you won your opponent's marble. Billy may have been poor in money, but he was rich in marbles.

I had the idea one summer day that if I could get Billy to the Hayes Pool, the free pool run by the city, maybe the chlorine would wash away some of the dirt and he wouldn't smell so bad. We walked along the railroad tracks, which was a shortcut to the pool. It wasn't really, but we pretended it was because one could always find interesting things along the tracks.

Billy wasn't feeling well. He said he had been hungry that morning and found some cupcakes in a box by the Nabisco factory. It really made him sick. As we made our way through the bushes alongside the track, Billy complained that he was getting diarrhea. "You keep guard," he said, as he looked for a concealed spot to relieve himself. I waited for several minutes, and then Billy whispered, "Is there any paper around?" "No. I don't see any." "Well, look. See if you can find some rags or something." "I don't see anything, Billy."

I heard the rustling of the bushes. A few minutes later Billy emerged. "What did you use," I asked. Billy grinned, "I used some of the leaves."

It was more than a week later that I saw Billy again. "Where've you been?" I inquired. "Home," he said, "I was hurting real bad. Still hurts a lot."

"From eating those cupcakes?"

"No, you dummy. From wiping my ass with poison sumac."

I never saw Billy after that summer. His grandmother died and he moved away with his father. I had heard recently that he was working for the health department in one of the shore communities.

The child is father to the man. What we live through makes us who we are. Our childhood is often the crucible in which is forged the strength that carries us through the rest of our lives, providing we are able to burn away the flaws. George Bernard Shaw observed that "youth is wasted on the young." But we need this time of trial and error to prepare for the best that is yet to come.

# THE RAT SAFARI

Peanut butter and jelly sandwiches in hand, we made our weekly Saturday morning excursions into new adventures in the urban wilderness that was the Newark of the fifties. For kids living in the city there was always something new to explore, and when you lived in a closed environment like a four-room apartment on the third floor, Mom was always glad when you got lost for the day. If you had a good imagination, you could go anywhere.

Sometimes we packed for a safari to Port Newark, to those areas where raw sewage was spread out to dry before being scooped up and sold for fertilizer. We went there because the rats were big and easier to hit with our BB guns. One day I brought along my bow and a quiver of eight arrows: six target and two hunting. I don't know why a ten-year old living in the city would want hunting arrows, but I was impressed with its large triangular head and razor-sharp blades. I could imagine myself hunting deer upstate somewhere, or maybe buffalo on the western plains. Robin Hood would have had arrows such as these. They were magnificent, but expensive—$1.20 a piece at Hunt's Sporting Goods on Market Street. I never used them, saving them for the day when I would take them on a real safari to Africa.

The field arrows were good enough for rats—and there were a lot of them. Billy and Angelo had BB guns. Angelo was pretty good with one. (Fifteen years later he died in a gunfight with the cops.) Sal found a long stick with a piece of metal on it. He said he would bash the crap out of any rat that got close to him, but he wouldn't get near to one with a ten foot pole.

Billy drew first blood. We saw the hit, but the rat escaped into a pile of boards. We then walked past some abandoned cars, and that's when I saw a big, ferocious snarling rat about fifteen feet away. I put my arm out to stop the others from going any further, and, like a Zen archer, the arrow was out of the quiver, onto the string, and launched without thinking or aiming. But it hit the mark and I was more surprised than any of them.

We watched as the rodent squealed for a brief moment, its blood oozing out from around the wooden shaft. His mouth opened and closed and then opened again in one last paroxysm of life. We stood in silence at the mystery of the departure of life and the finality of death. It didn't matter that this was a rat. It had been a living thing and I had taken its life. We stood there somewhat in awe of our power and feeling guilty for playing God. Angelo broke the silence—"I'm hungry. Let's eat."

I never wanted to kill anything again. I left the arrow there in the rat corpse and perhaps gave a fleeting thought that I would spend the rest of my life atoning for that death.

John Donne may have been right—"Any man's death diminishes me because I am involved in mankind." But what about a rat? Am I less of a person because of a rodent death? Albert Schweitzer would say so. The sanctity of life in any form is precious. We know that we should not take human life, but what of animals—elephants, whales, horses, dogs, rats, mosquitos? Where do we draw the line? And what about living organic matter? Apples and carrots? Do I dare to eat a peach? Should I become a Jainist and wear a mask over my mouth and nose so that I don't unintentionally inhale an insect?

I have come to learn that all life is precious, but like the energy of the universe, life is not destroyed. It is only transformed and will find expression again in another time or place. If I am the less for anyone's death, or for the death of any of God's creatures, it is because I have established a relationship with that life and have given meaning to that life in my own. When I am aware of my connection with the universe, I am aware that all things have meaning to each other. And all things exist for the sake of one another, whether we are aware of it or not.

That is especially true of us humans. I may not know the elderly Chinese farmer eking out a meager existence among the countless millions of his countrymen, or the Peruvian Indian high in the Andes, but somehow their lives have meaning for my own. I can only hope that their experiences will be shared with my own in some future time when we are all together in the mind of God. Until that occurs I will respect the lives of others—and all things, including rats.

# SATURDAY MATINEE AT THE RIVOLI

CHILDREN HAVE A TOUGH life. From the perspective of adulthood it doesn't seem so. What do children have to worry about compared with making a living, getting along with your spouse, your family, your neighbors, dealing with institutions of various kinds? I sometimes look at my cat lounging around all day, having me to feed him, put out his water, change his litter box, pet him. I get downright resentful. Why doesn't he do something to justify his existence?

And then I think that he does. He exists for me to serve his needs and in turn he gives me unconditional love. And that seems to be enough.

But in a child's world there are all kinds of fears and anxieties. Children worry about whether they are loved and cared for. Sometimes they worry if there will be enough to eat. They sometimes live in terror that their father or mother won't be there to take care of them, that they might die and leave them alone in an uncaring world.

My childhood was spent in the post-war world. Hiroshima and Nagasaki had ushered in a new and terrifying future. In school we had air raid drills and had to march quickly to the basement and huddle against the corridor walls with our heads buried in our hands. We were told about what radiation could do to a person and that in the event of an attack it might be weeks before water and food would be available. I saw the room where emergency provisions were stockpiled for that eventuality. School assemblies reinforced the dangers of the nuclear age, and some of my classmates spoke about their fathers building bomb shelters in the back yard. Since we didn't have one in our yard, my family would never survive. I lived with that constant fear and cringed every time the sirens would go off for a drill.

The nuclear nightmare that characterized the fifties was bad enough, but at any time any one of us could also be stricken with the dreaded polio. We knew of children spending their lives in iron lungs. Those, like President Roosevelt, who were only crippled were luckier than most. But we all thought polio or cancer or muscular dystrophy or tuberculosis might get us. It seemed that every month there was a collection in school for one disease or another, and the teachers made us feel that if we didn't bring in our nickels and dimes we would get that particular disease. I had learned about more afflictions through these campaigns than anyplace else, and I had also acquired new fears.

One of the real fears in elementary school that occasionally would be justified was the fear of getting beat up by the class bully when you left school. If I didn't give Orlando my lunch money or the answers to the homework assignment, I could expect to hear the same words: "I'll get you after school." There were many times that I would try to leave by a door at the opposite end of the building, and sometimes I would deliberately get into trouble just so that the teacher would give me detention.

In my early childhood, my refuge was not so much the church, but the movie house. Most likely it fulfilled the same function that television does today, offering a magic window into a fantasy world that could be every bit as real as the one that was fraught with so many dangers and snares. The Rivoli on Ferry Street was our sanctuary, and for twenty cents one could spend all day Saturday in the dark confines of another world.

It was a real world. The first time my grandfather took me to the movies, I must have been about four years old. I only remember a restaurant scene with elegantly dressed people seated at small round tables with little lamps on them. It was so real, even though it was in black and white, that I walked up onto the stage and began touching the table on the screen, except that it disappeared as I blocked the projected image. I remember the laughter from the audience mixed with some yelling to get that kid out of there. My grandfather got to me before an usher did and escorted me back to my seat. But I was hooked.

The ushers were like demi-gods—some would say devils—in the cavernous darkness of the theater. They wore uniforms and carried flashlights as symbols of their authority, and they could throw you out of the movie if you misbehaved. We tried to avoid them as much as possible. There was one time when I saw an usher's power diminish right in front of me. He was shining his light on some kids in the row in front of me and telling them

## SATURDAY MATINEE AT THE RIVOLI

to come with him. He was going to throw them out, but at the crucial moment, the batteries in his flashlight failed and his light went out. The kids scrambled every which way, and the usher was powerless since he could not identify any of them.

The Rivoli was a small movie theater, but much larger than today's intimate box-like cinemas. It was large enough for East Side High School to hold their commencement exercises here before they built their new auditorium. But compared to the huge movie palaces uptown, it was small. Newark boasted more than a dozen cinemas in just a five block radius in the middle of the city. There was a theater for each of the major studios, and they showed only the films produced by that studio. Each had its own characteristics. The Paramount was impressive because of its gigantic lobby and two-story staircase. The Proctors was six stories tall and ran elevators just like Radio City. The Branford had two entrances, one of which was hidden in an alley, but it was a large theater. And Lowe's, across from Military Park, was ornately decorated inside. It was especially noted for its publicity gimmicks. When the movie *The Thing* was shown, the front pavement had its footprints leading inside, and slime was smeared under the marquis. My mother had given me money to see this movie, but as soon as I saw those footprints I caught the next bus home.

The movies provided us with our heroes and role models. Errol Flynn was the most popular. Whenever Errol appeared with his sword and leotards, you can imagine the number of swashbuckling adventures that were enacted on the way home. Every stray broomstick and ash can cover was seized as the duel with the evil Sheriff of Nottingham was refought with gusto and loud clangor.

Johnny Weissmuller was also a favorite. The merchants on Ferry Street must have hated those Tarzan movies, because the kids would swing on their awnings as they made their way home. I saw many bent awning poles inflicted by the fat kids. In the winter we risked the danger of colds whenever a Batman or Superman movie was shown. That's when we would take our coats off and tie them around our necks like capes. I had heard that one faux-Superman had broken his leg in a fall from a high stoop, but when we had our capes on we always believed we were invincible.

The westerns were the best. Whenever a Hopalong Cassidy, Roy Rogers, or Gene Autry movie was playing, we would strap our guns to our waists and mosey on down to the Rivoli. We liked Hoppy the best—he didn't sing or kiss his horse, and he was always a nice guy, even when he had to kill someone.

My mother took me uptown to Bamberger's Department Store to see Roy Rogers one day. We got on the bus and there were a lot of other kids with guns and Roy Rogers shirts. I felt undressed because I didn't have my guns with me—what was Roy going to say? It seemed like hours that we waited in a line that wound through the store past everything that the marketing professionals wanted to sell to young mothers, and also through the toy department. But I finally got to meet Roy. There was also Dale Evans and Gabby Hayes and even Trigger. As I patted Trigger's mane I could just picture Roy riding this beautiful palomino up the escalator. What a wonderful sight that must have been. When Roy said "Howdy, pardner" to me, I was dumbstruck. There was so much I wanted to say to him, but I had to keep moving along. When Dale and Gabby both said, "Howdy, pardner," not only to me but to the boy in back of me, I wondered how many "pardners" they had. It was no longer just me alone.

I never got that close to Gene Autry. I shook his hand once at a rodeo in Madison Square Garden, but most of the attention was being given to an Indian in the stands a few rows from me. I noticed a lot of people running over to him with pieces of paper and he was writing something on them. I asked my uncle who that was and he said, "That's Jim Thorpe. Why don't you get his autograph?" I didn't know who Jim Thorpe was at the time and I would rather shake hands with Gene Autry. I still regret that missed opportunity, but I remember Thorpe's face very well. Many years later I visited his grave in the Pennsylvania town that bears his name. I said silently, "Sorry. Jim, I didn't know who you were." I could hear a voice within me say, "That's okay. I'm still learning who I am."

I knew that I was emerging from childhood when I went to see Marlon Brando in *On the Waterfront*. I had grown up around longshoremen, so this was nothing new. Tony Galento was in the movie. I had met him once; I think he had some boxing connection with my father. Two-Ton Tony, unlike Brando's character, had been a contender for the heavyweight title and had stunned Joe Louis with a knockdown punch in his losing effort. I went to the evening show—I had grown beyond matinees—and when I came out of the theater, there was Tony standing at the curb pouring the last of his popcorn into his mouth. "Hi, Tony," I said. "How ya doin' kid?" he replied. This was no longer fantasy; this was reality. The character had come down from the screen.

# THE RESTORER OF SOULS

CHILDHOOD FEARS HAVE A way of influencing our preferences in later years. We may take an instant dislike to people we have never before known just because a physical or behavioral characteristic conjures a latent memory of someone from the distant past with whom we may have had an unpleasant relationship.

Mike the shoemaker was not an unpleasant man. He had his shop on Magazine Street, around the corner from where we lived on Marne Street. He was an immigrant (from Poland, or Germany, or Hungary—I don't remember), but he came in pursuit of the American dream. Lucas would take me with him whenever he had a pair of shoes to be resoled or heels to be replaced. It was fun to watch Mike at his machinery, especially the long lathe-like apparatus with its assorted buffers and grinders and belts and pulleys. It made a noise like a huge factory.

Sometimes I would watch Mike use the stitching machine. I remember him telling Grandpa that back in the old country he used to make lots of riding boots for rich people. I wondered what kind of cars these people had that they needed special shoes to ride in them. He laughed and asked me if I had ever seen a horse. Of course I had—cops and cowboys had them. He laughed again and made some remark about kids in America not knowing how good they had it compared to those who lived through the war.

As a six-year old I didn't understand what he was talking about, but I had felt that he was making fun of me, and I didn't like it. Another customer came in and Mike came to the counter where all the pairs of finished shoes were lined up with tickets sticking out of them waiting for their owners. I thought he was a little gruff when he asked me to get out of the way so he could find the customer's shoes.

## THE DWELLING PLACE OF WONDER

When Mike turned his back to go to the register, I saw the large can of glue on the small table that he used to repair soles (for years I had thought that line in Psalm 23, "he restoreth my soul," referred to shoemakers). I casually picked up the glue can and inverted it as I walked toward the door, taking care to pour the glue into every pair of shoes on the counter. When I heard Mike's loud yell of anger and bewilderment, I dropped the can and ran out of the shop.

It was years before I would dare to turn the corner onto Magazine Street. Even as a teenager I felt a deep sense of guilt over this childhood deed, and although Mike has long since closed his shop, I still feel the pangs of conscience whenever I see the building.

I sometimes can imagine Mike laughing about this years later, but for the most part his angry scowl and piercing yell were imbedded in my memory. Fear had long since turned to remorse as I felt sorry for the extra work I had put this immigrant cobbler through. Mike would never know as he cleaned those shoes that my soul would not be restored for many years to come, and that he would determine how I would be impressed by strangers decades later.

It's too late to ask Mike to forgive the impulsive behavior of a six-year-old. But I can imagine him forgiving me and that is enough to lift the burden. Some seeds take a long time to bear their fruit.

I was to see the pain of guilt and the need for forgiveness many times in my life: a young German man seeking absolution in Jerusalem, a depressed youth leader taking on the sins of the world and blowing his brains out with a shotgun blast, a tough truck driver blaming himself for his son's accidental drowning.

One of my parishioners, Barry, had killed a man. Not intentionally, but the man was dead nevertheless. The twenty-year-old had stepped in front of Barry's pickup on some back road in Northampton County. It didn't help much when the police administered the requisite breathalyzer test and found that Barry was just over the limit—one beer too many.

It was not his first DUI and Barry had to spend some time in county prison. They used to call them "penitentiaries," places where one was to become penitent by having time to think about one's sinful ways. Later they were called "correctional centers." I suppose "behavioral modification facility" might be another euphemism. They were names used in the hope that the one incarcerated would turn out to be a better person when released than when admitted.

# THE RESTORER OF SOULS

For Barry, prison was a place of confinement, and when he was released he went straight to the nearest bar. The bartender called a cab and sent him home to his parent's house. In the years following he was seldom sober, but he never drove again. Pursued by the Furies for the "killing," as he called it, he sought oblivion in the hardest liquor he could find.

It didn't take long. His mother, Ethel, one of our faithful workers in the church, came to me and said that her son was dying. The cirrhosis had progressed to the point where his liver was hardly working. She wanted me to visit him.

I had never seen a person that yellow. Barry stared at me through jaundiced eyes and finally spoke. "I'm sorry," he said, "for all that I put my mother through. I know that the people at the church were praying for me, and I let them down. When I was a little boy, I went to Sunday school and church every week, and when I was confirmed I promised God that I would remain faithful. I guess I failed him too. Or maybe he failed me by letting these things happen."

Before I could assure him of God's love and forgiveness, Barry made his final request: "You know, I always went to the Ash Wednesday service to receive the ashes on my forehead. For some reason that meant an awful lot to me. God was putting his black mark on me, but it took me a while to realize that it was a sign of God's mercy and forgiveness. When I die, I want to be cremated, and I want you to add my ashes to those that you use on Ash Wednesday. I want all those people in the church to know that God has forgiven me, and I hope they will too."

I couldn't accept the thought of "all those people" wearing Barry on their foreheads, so I made no promise, and didn't do it. But I did share the story of a man who held an intense desire to receive the love and forgiveness of God and of the community of faith, and who in the end returned from the far country and was welcomed home by a waiting Father. In the end, our souls are restored to a loving God.

# "HELLO DARKNESS, MY OLD FRIEND"

On my first day at summer camp I knew that it would be an entirely different experience. I arrived after midnight. The director's flashlight guided my feet through the dark woods. The sounds of the forest were frightening to those of us from the city who were used to police sirens, screeching brakes, landing jets at the Newark Airport, and the domestic squabbling of the neighbors.

For me the eerie silence was comforting. It took a while to realize that in the absence of city noise to which I had grown accustomed, there were other sounds that were gentler, more rhythmic, like the sound of a pulsing heart that, when heard in the absence of all other sounds, lets you know that you are alive.

They didn't turn on the lights in the cabin, but told me to get into bed as quietly as possible. All things will be settled in the morning. It was a long drive from Newark to these Pennsylvania woods. I had been told that when I crossed the Delaware I would be on the frontier of civilization, in a land of farms and cows where strange men with beards dressed in simple black clothes and rode in buggies. I couldn't think of that now. My tired ten-year-old body just wanted to sleep, but in my fading consciousness I heard the deafening sounds of crickets, the water of a swift running stream hitting hard against the stones, and the night breeze moving a branch against the screened window. It was a sylvan symphony in counterpoint to yesterday's urban cacophony, but also a prelude to a desperate need for order and balance in my life.

## "HELLO DARKNESS, MY OLD FRIEND"

I have never been afraid of the dark, only of what might happen in the dark—not unlike the traveler who said he had no fear of flying, but only of crashing. I had long since learned to befriend the darkness. It was a place of refuge and calm.

The earliest memories that I have of this life were in the third-floor apartment above a shoe store on Wilson Avenue that my parents moved into after they were married in Maryland. It was a sparsely furnished flat with hardly any furniture. I had no crib as a baby, but slept in the bottom drawer of a chest. The room was dimly lit by a single bare bulb in the ceiling. I got use to the shadows. Sometimes at night I would crawl out of my drawer to look out the window on a winter's night to watch the snow accumulate on the cobbled street. Below our window was a metal chest filled with sand that trolley drivers might need to provide traction when the rails became too slippery. The street lamp illuminated the dark gray box and created a vivid impression against the white snow. Even at that early age I had the feeling of loneliness.

Mr. and Mrs. George Miller lived down the hall. As my godparents, they kept an eye on me, but not very well. I was known to crawl out the back window onto the garage roof. It was a different perspective on the world from that of the apartment rooms, but it drew a lot of attention from passersby. Apparently they thought a toddler alone on a roof might come to some harm. I couldn't understand the fuss, but welcomed the attention.

My father taught me about darkness and light. The dark was not always evil and the light was not always good. Throughout my childhood, Dad was an occasional visitor. He had no permanent residence in my life. The apartments where we lived were merely the walk-in closets where he changed his clothes and paid his lip-service to fatherhood. Nevertheless, his visitations were occasions to be celebrated and relished. Sometimes he came like the magi bearing strange and wonderful gifts—a bag of silver dollars from the slot machines in Vegas or a boxer puppy someone had given him or a stack of comic books.

I would look forward to these unannounced arrivals and was disappointed if I saw a stogie in the ash tray—the sign of his presence—but missed him. These epiphanies were joyous indeed compared to the days of wrath that seemed far more frequent. I had no fear of the tongue-lashing that I might receive for some childhood indiscretion. Certainly I had committed enough sins that my churlish behavior was considered normal. If I had been a Catholic like the rest of my family, my mother would have sent me off to confession with a bag-lunch.

My father was tolerant of my behavior. I wish I could have been more tolerant of his. It was only much later that I realized that while I was beginning my childhood, he was just ending his. He had not yet learned to deal with his emotions, or to control them.

Some of his visits were psycho-dramas played out like a Tennessee Williams play. How I wished we could have afforded pewter tableware or restricted those parental discussions with Mom to an arena free of throwable objects. While other children would lie secure in their beds, I would wake up at three o'clock in the morning to loud shouts and the clatter of dishes breaking against the wall.

These were the times when I welcomed the darkness and constructed out of my bedcovers a deep cavern into which I could retreat. I would think of the words of the hymn we sang at church: "Rock of Ages cleft for me, let me hide myself in Thee." How often did I want to find that rock and hide myself in it, protected from the raging battles and skirmishes to which children are sometimes subjected.

Time has a way of putting all things in perspective. That's why nostalgia is so wonderful and why we always want to go back to the past. Not only can we remember it the way we want to, but we know how it turned out, and that we have survived and prevailed.

My mom and dad fell in love, got married, fought their battles, got to know each other and themselves, graduated from their relationship, and went on to other lives. It's not the way I would have scripted it, but then it wasn't my play. I only had a cameo appearance, a walk-on. I have my own play to write, but I am grateful for the shadows, for it is in the darkness that seeds germinate and growth begins.

# NEWSPAPERS

Bob Nackley approached me with a business proposition that he guaranteed would set me on the path to a lucrative career in the newspaper business. He was a district manager for the *Newark News* and appealed to my entrepreneurial spirit and my need for financial subsistence. Though I was only twelve years old at the time and my financial needs were modest, Bob convinced me that the experience of delivering newspapers would greatly assist in the development of my character by teaching me responsibility. I would learn communication and management skills and get in the newspaper business at the ground level. After all, Thomas Edison and many other notable Americans got their start selling the news.

My territory was an interracial neighborhood of predominantly Italians and African Americans with a smattering of Eastern Europeans and Portuguese. Most lived in three-story apartment buildings that were generally run down but clean. There were a few that were creaky and dirty with no light in the halls. I subcontracted the scarier tenements to my younger brother, George, who benefitted by developing his fearless nature.

It was a learning experience. I delivered an evening paper that often arrived at the door at the same time husbands were coming home from work and wives were in the midst of preparing dinner. It was often a time of confrontation, the flash point for domestic violence. The pent-up frustrations of the work-place collided with those of the school and the home. Moving through the halls of the apartment buildings, I could hear the domestic fights and petty squabbling, occasionally loud yelling and the crash of dishes. Once on a stairwell I heard a gunshot and ran down the steps so fast that I tripped out the door.

Newspaper carriers were sometimes called upon for service above and beyond the normal routine of delivering papers. Sometimes we were asked to run errands. Mrs. Albanese once sent me to the fish market at Ferry and Monroe. The boy behind the counter didn't wrap the fish too tightly and it squeezed out of the newspaper on to my polo shirt. The smell was so bad I had to take it off and finish my route stripped to the waist.

Mrs. DeLuca was a very young housewife, but a big tipper. When her clothesline broke and she called on me to fix the problem, I thought that this was far above the call of duty in delivering newspapers. She assured me that the solution was relatively simple and quite safe, and that I would be amply rewarded. It was just a matter of climbing a three-story pole and attaching a reel to a hook. It was probably the most foolish thing I had done in my life, but my manhood was in question and the financial gain very tempting. So I did it. My hands were bloodied from clinging so tightly to the spikes. My pants were ripped, torn by protruding nails. My arms were filled with splinters, and my shirt was covered with grease. Mrs. DeLuca was so grateful that she gave me a quarter. I stared at the quarter, and then at Mrs. DeLuca. She said, "What's the matter? Isn't that enough?" and then began to undo the top two buttons of her blouse. I said, "I'll take the quarter," and hurriedly left the apartment. I quickly learned that acts of kindness are their own reward.

I also learned how people dealt with disabilities. Mr. Albanese lost an arm in the war and used a prosthesis. The first time I went to collect from him he "handed" me a dollar bill pinched between the clamps of his device. He laughed as I reluctantly and very gingerly took the dollar from him and told me to keep the change.

The Quintos were both deaf. When you pressed the doorbell outside their apartment, a light would go on inside so that they would know you were there. When they opened a door, they would turn on another light in the corridor so that they could read your lips when you spoke to them. If I was short a paper, I would rather go to the store and buy one rather than miss them. They depended so much upon the printed word to maintain their contact with the world.

There were customers that were so disgusting and repulsive that you would just as soon not collect from them. An eighty-year-old grandmother always answered the door in her bra and wanted me to come inside while she looked for the money. I felt sorry for Mr. Neto, who had a skin disease that made him look like a creature from a horror flick; every time I knocked

# NEWSPAPERS

on his door I hoped that Mrs. Neto would answer. Tony Giordano was a longshoreman. He was okay, but he kept his big longshoreman's hook right next to the door. It was intimidating. One day I heard him shouting at his wife and I looked and saw that the hook was missing. The image of a dead body lying on the kitchen floor with a slashed torso came immediately to mind—another picture filed away in the memory banks to add to the nightmares of childhood.

Father Kanopic was the autocratic pastor of St. Casimir's. Whatever reputation he enjoyed among his parishioners I saw him as stern and aloof, especially since I frequently saw him in his cassock and biretta. He was conservative and he was cheap. I always tried to time my collections at the rectory when I knew the younger priests were more likely to answer. Even when they did and Father Kanopic was in residence, he told them how much of tip they should give.

I had been reading a book on Egyptology and came across the term "canopic jars"—jars that were used to preserve the organs of dead Egyptians. When one of the young priests answered the door the next week, I asked him if he knew that canopic jars were containers for dead organs. He laughed as he slowly closed the door and said, "Very apt. Very apt."

Delivering the papers provided little windows into the lives of other families. Some made me envious; others helped me appreciate my own situation. More than anything else, I encountered a great variety of human beings who were not only physically different, but complex in their psychological makeup. What made some people predisposed to violent behavior while others almost always acted with kindness? Why were some people friendly and others distant, some caring and others disinterested? It took time, but eventually I recognized that everyone had an empty place in their lives, and how they reacted to other people was a call to fulfill that need. We are all lonely people in some way, and the loneliest are often those who live closest to others.

# EYES ON THE STEEPLE

Before he became my uncle, "Johnny Bones" sat with the kids on the front porch on Monroe Street. We lived for a time in a third-floor apartment on a street with only one other house. Dominated by the Newark Rivet Works across the street and the Vitamin Corporation of America on the corner, our section of Monroe Street was often deserted and, on dark summer nights, rather quiet for a city street.

While Aunt Angie would look after my two younger brothers, Johnny would engage in intellectual repartee as befitting the pre-teen group, such as seeing how many cowboys we could name, or whether the New York Yankees or the Brooklyn Dodgers had the better lineup. (For some reason no one much cared about the Giants, in spite of Willie Mays.)

As the night progressed, the conversation inevitably turned to ghosts and monsters. Johnny seemed to be an authority on vampires and werewolves. His stories were richly embellished to the point where we had a difficult time going to sleep. We tried to imagine that our blankets had some magical power to protect us.

The Lon Chaney Jr. werewolf movies were fresh in our minds, and our gang decided to go to Independence Park to make sure that there was no wolfsbane growing there. Never mind that we had no idea what it looked like, we wanted to be sure that it would not accidentally fall into the wrong hands and induce a lycanthropic transformation. Every one of us could recite the lines from the old gypsy: "Even those who are pure of heart, and say their prayers at night, can become a wolf, when the wolfsbane blooms and the autumn moon is bright."

Werewolves didn't bother us near as much as vampires, and, while we didn't put pouches of garlic around our necks as vampire repellant, we did sharpen some wooden stakes in the cellar. I had heard that waving a crucifix at a vampire would scare him away, but Johnny squashed that idea by asking, "What if he's Jewish?"

John had just finished telling us the story of the Mummy's Curse and putting tanna leaves in our hands (I think he just tore open a tea bag) when two young women came running around the corner yelling something about seeing red eyes on the steeple of St. James Church. St. James's was the territorial Roman Catholic church around the block from us, between Madison and Jefferson Streets. We could see the very tip of its spire from our house. The women claimed that they had seen a pair of fiery eyes moving about the steeple as if looking for something or someone.

Always interested in the mysterious, we left the porch and hurried to Madison Street to join a group of about a dozen or so men, women, and children scouring the church for a glimpse of the red eyes. A man shouted, "Look, there it is!" When our eyes focused on the spot to which the man pointed, it was gone. Another said, "There, in the school window," referring to the parochial school in back.

While I saw nothing, I could not doubt that the others believed that they had seen something peculiar. Would careful investigation reveal some natural phenomena like reflections from the tail lights of passing cars? Was it a matter of wanting to see the unusual so much that the mind invents that which the heart desires?

Years later, as I came to distinguish between the campfire ghost stories told as entertainment, and the apparition sightings of credible witnesses, the entire issue of Biblical miracles came into question. Were all the miracle stories from the Old Testament and from the life of Jesus misinterpretations of ordinary phenomena by true believers, or were they figments of desire created in the brain, bypassing the mechanisms of sight and sound?

Did the women at the tomb of Jesus mistake him for the gardener as the gospel relates, or was the reverse true? Was it really the gardener that the women wanted to believe was Jesus? The questions would come: Did it really happen? Was the reporting accurate? Were there other explanations? How could two millennia of Christian faith hang by the single thread of a false observation or misinterpretation?

The truth is that we live by faith regardless of the truth. We act on what we believe even though there may be no basis in fact. When my mother was a teenager, she was with some friends when she heard about the Martian landing at Grovers Mill, some forty miles away. It was on the news, someone said. There was no panic, but there was fear and concern as the group quickly dispersed to run home and be with loved ones should the aliens attack the city of Newark as they made their way to the metropolis across the river. Of course, she learned later that it was only a Mercury Theater of the Air dramatization of H. G. Wells's *War of the Worlds*. In spite of repeated announcements by Orson Welles that it was only a fabrication, many were convinced of its reality. The gathering storm of war in Europe had produced its own anxiety and set the stage for mass hysteria.

There are degrees of believability. Some stories are so fantastic that everyone, except perhaps little children, knows them to be fairy tales. Add enough elements of known fact so that the story could be true and you increase its plausibility. Suspend reason sufficiently and you have a credible account upon which a person is prepared to act.

My wife, Mary Ann, and I spent most every summer visiting Mary Ann's brother at Wrightsville Beach, North Carolina. Bill had lived in the state for a number of years working as a nuclear engineer for General Electric. He was a scientist trained in the empirical method. Ghost stories were simply that—curious tales told for amusement. You believed in them only to the point of being entertained on a quiet night as you watched the lights along the shore.

North Carolina has more than its share of ghost stories and I was particularly interested in those centered around Wilmington. The story of Joe Baldwin and the ghost light at Maco Station was of particular interest. Joe Baldwin had been a railroad conductor on the Atlantic Coast Line. One night in 1867, he made his way through the train to the last car, which was empty. Perhaps it was his weight stepping into the car or a sudden bump that caused the car to become uncoupled from the rest of the train. As the car gradually slowed, Joe became aware of another train following on the same track. He frantically waved his lantern in a desperate attempt to signal the pursuing locomotive. The crash was horrendous and according to the stories, Joe's head was severed from his body. They found Joe, but not his head.

For many years thereafter a ghostly light was seen along the tracks near Maco Station. It was believed to be Joe looking for his head. The phenomenon occurred with such regularity that the railroad ordered its trainmen to use two lanterns, one red and one green, so as not to be confused by the Baldwin light.

When Bill's son, Alan, moved to a house near Maco Station, we thought it might be fun to go out to the section of track where the light was generally seen. It was a hot, sultry night in August, but there was a group of persons already there waiting for the light to appear. While some thought that they had spotted it some distance down the track, most of us agreed that perhaps Joe decided it was just too hot to be out looking for his head.

We were about ready to call it a night when Mary Ann said, "Wait. I think I sense something." We grew quiet as Mary Ann listened to the voice within her telling her that it was Baldwin himself, and that he thought it was silly that people would believe that he was looking for his head. Mary Ann learned from Joe that he had been married and had a daughter. She sensed their presence and was able to describe their dress and hair style. Joe indicated that the light was a lingering vestige of a traumatic event.

The next day we visited the New Hanover Library and were permitted to see contemporary newspaper accounts of the incident which were kept in a file folder. We were surprised to read that Joe Baldwin was survived by a wife and daughter, confirming the revelation of the previous night which had not been known to us prior to our visit to Maco Station.

Ghost stories often consist of what we bring to them, the machinations of our own mind and a readiness to accept the fantastic against all reason. The mind is a sometimes devious mechanism. It often sees what it wants to see, and creates a reality with which the person is comfortable and can operate in safety. While Augustine and Anselm said that we must believe in order to see (*credo ut intelligam*), science wants us to see in order to believe. But there is some truth in Anaïs Nin's comment, "We don't see things as they are; we see things as we are."

Just how important is belief to understanding? Do we accept the anecdotal material gathered by researchers, the inexplicable video and audio impressions, the recollections of children that suggest a previous life, the vast library of myth, legend, religious fable, and other outpourings of the human mind and experience as evidence that there is something more that exists beyond our knowing and beyond scientific verification?

I believe that we do. While the veridical evidence of science seeks to uncover signs of the transcendent, there is also an element of the human psyche that not only wants to believe that there is more to life than we can see, but intuitively "knows" that there is.

Humans fear death, not so much because we do not know what dreams may come, but because we are afraid that there will be no dreams. Joseph

Campbell revised his definition of myth from the "search for meaning" to the "experience of life." All of the stories we have heard throughout our lives about apparitions, psychic phenomena, "strange visitors from another planet," the fabrications of the mind, episodes from a "galaxy far, far away," after-death visions, and so on, all form the corpus of our life experience. When we examine the entire body of literature of the mind reaching beyond itself, we know that we are more than what we appear to be.

An old anonymous Aztec poem says, "We come but to sleep, we come but to dream: It is not true, it is not true, that we come to live upon the earth." And yet, in our dreaming we are alive. Before we can bring into the physical world the manifestation of love, we have to dream it, conceive it, and give birth to it.

There are times when we simply must walk by faith and not by sight, when we must push beyond the normal, slip the surly bonds of earthbound thinking, and stretch beyond our grasp. Sometimes we must simply believe the unbelievable.

# THE CHURCH OF THE VANISHING JESUS

THE CHURCH OF MY youth was destroyed in the Martian invasion that took place in the early years of the twenty-first century. Its steeple came crashing down into Ferry Street when the aliens surfaced from beneath the street as frightened residents scattered before the onslaught of the deadly rays.

Steven Spielberg had used St. Stephan's United Church of Christ in Newark as his headquarters while filming *War of the Worlds*. While much of the destruction was computer generated, it was nevertheless disconcerting to see my church crumble into dust.

St. Stephan's is an imposing landmark in the Ironbound section of Newark, New Jersey. It was constructed so as to dominate the intersection where Ferry Street, the main thoroughfare, bears left as it heads in the direction of Manhattan. In the early days of Newark, this was the road that went through a narrow neck of swampland to meet the ferries that crossed the Hudson River to New York City. Old-timers still refer to the Ironbound as "Down-Neck."

As to the name "Ironbound," the section was bounded by the iron rails of the Pennsylvania and Central Railroad of New Jersey. One could not enter the area without crossing over or under the tracks. In the early years of the twentieth century, many of the sections of Newark had distinctive ethnic groups. The Italians settled near Branch Brook Park, the Jews in the Weequahic section, and the black population dominated the central and south side sections. The Ironbound, the east side, was the German section, with streets named for German cities like Bremen, Berlin, and Hamburg. In a frenzy of anti-German feelings during the First World War, Bremen Street became Marne Street, Hamburg Place became Wilson Avenue, and Berlin was superseded by Rome.

Following the war, the Ironbound became the great melting pot. The Italian enclave grew and clustered around Independence Park where the Dutch bowling greens became bocce courts. Other ethnic groups were scattered throughout the section but generally gathered around their churches and their particular saints. While the Italians had their Lady of Mount Carmel, the Irish had St. Aloysius, the Poles St. Casimir's on Pulaski Street, Our Lady of Fatima for the Portuguese, and the German Catholics worshipped at St. Benedict's (commonly called "St. Bendix"). Other churches served the spiritual needs of Lithuanians, Russians, Greeks, and Dutch.

St. Stephan's Church was special. There are not many congregations that have been founded because its members wanted to have beer at their meetings, or where Jesus turns his back whenever any minister tries to preach in his name. And yet, like the little brown church in the wildwood, it was the place of precious memories and spiritual formation.

The church was founded in 1874 when Oscar H. Kraft, a former Union officer, gathered some eighty families together to discuss the idea of establishing a congregation that would be united with the Evangelical Church, a denomination formed in Germany in 1815 by the union of Reformed and Lutheran people. The oral tradition has it that many German Lutherans had settled in Newark and worked in the more than a dozen breweries that were located in the city. (A century ago the water was more palatable than it is now.) These German braumeisters had joined the local Presbyterian church, but when that congregation adopted a resolution calling for strict temperance, the Germans, who loved their brew, were forced into a moral dilemma. The solution was to form a church that allowed the use of beer. (For many years the elder in charge of consistory meetings would see to it that pitchers of beer were placed on the tables.)

At eight o'clock in the evening on St. Patrick's Day, a group met with Pastor Kraft in a carpenter shop on Van Buren Street and adopted a constitution. They named their church after the first Christian martyr who was stoned in Jerusalem. The following month the young congregation was accepted as a member of the Evangelical Synod of North America with the official name "The German United Evangelical St. Stephan's Church." An impressive edifice was designed by George Staehlin in a Romanesque style with a Georgian steeple. Appropriately, the Hensler Brewery, located a block away, contributed substantially to the interior decor.

# THE CHURCH OF THE VANISHING JESUS

St. Stephan's grew rapidly in size to over 2,000 members under the leadership of Pastor Edward Fuhrmann and his son, Edward W. Furhmann. Their two pastorates spanned a fifty year period from 1897 to 1947. In those years when the German language was still used for worship and frequently for conversation among the leadership, there was a growing separation between the older generation of founding fathers and their Americanized sons and daughters. The minister was still "Herr Pastor," and was treated with the respect due to one who was a step removed from God. On the other hand, blasphemy was quite common as some of the more cantankerous older group often voiced their disagreements with the pastoral leadership.

One of the unusual features of the church was its large, ornate, enclosed pulpit. Its central and elevated position above the altar emphasized the importance of the sermon in worship. Since "faith comes from what is heard, and what is heard comes through the word of Christ" (Romans 10:17), preaching was dominant in the congregation's tradition.

To make sure that it was the word of the Lord that was emanating from the pulpit, there was a large statue of Christ, with hands outstretched, mounted on a pedestal affixed to the rear panel of the pulpit. The panel was on a pivot that was turned by the preacher when he entered the pulpit. Most likely the intended theology was that the preacher stands in the place of Christ and speaks for Christ when delivering the sermon. The reality was that Jesus left whenever the pastor appeared, or that he turned his back on what was being said about him.

There was always something mysterious about Jesus leaving the pulpit. Usually during the preceding hymn, the pastor would rotate Jesus out of the pulpit as he ascended the steps to take his place. Since our eyes were often glued to the hymnal, we would miss this transformation, and when we looked up, we beheld the miracle of the vanishing Jesus and of his replacement. In the Middle Ages, the truly devout would run from church to church on Sunday mornings just to observe the elevation of the host and chalice so as to behold the miracle of the mass, the wonderful and mysterious transformation of the elements into the actual body and blood of Christ. Even though we understood what was happening, the vanishing Jesus was almost our miracle. It reminded me of the old Frank Sinatra movie, *The Miracle of the Bells*, where a statue turns to face the coffin of a dead actress. Explanations somehow do not diminish the wonder.

Matthew Theis was the first minister to come to St. Stephan's from the Reformed side of the merger with the Evangelical Synod of North America, being steeped in the Mercersburg Theology as taught at Lancaster Theological Seminary. He was horrified at the thought of being Jesus' supply or substitute preacher. He felt as if it he was saying, "Get thee behind me, Jesus." So he refused to ask Jesus to leave. It was better, he maintained, to have Jesus in back of him, bestowing his blessing upon the pastor's words.

Matt Theis was a large man, looking every bit like images of Martin Luther; and like Luther, he loved his beer. One Sunday morning he mounted the pulpit to stand in front of Jesus, but the two of them could not fit in the same space, and Matt accidentally broke the arms of the statue. The plaster Jesus was removed from the panel, and the next week Pastor Theis's sermon was, "Christ Has No Hands But Our Hands."

Jesus has been restored to his rightful place above the altar, but most of the recent pastors have chosen to preach from the lectern rather than ask Christ to leave.

I had never had a problem with the theology of the vanishing Jesus. It never bothered me that Jesus turned his back on the congregation. After all, Moses considered it a sublime spiritual experience when he visualized the divine derriere from his cleft in the rock.

Mercersburg Theology emphasized the sacrament of Holy Communion as the outward and visible sign of the presence of Christ among us and the primary focus of the church's worship. The Incarnation was a central ingredient of the faith, for not only was God manifest in Jesus of Nazareth, but God is still present and speaking in the world today. Matt Theis was right: Jesus does not leave us but is in us as we live out the Christ-like life. Nevertheless, while I don't require the presence of a statue to remind me of that, somehow the departure of the physical Jesus emphasized the continuing work of the Holy Spirit through his disciples. And yet, the outstretched and welcoming arms of a loving Christ embracing all God's children was very comforting.

# IT STARTED WITH A COFFEE CAN

I HAVE LEARNED MUCH from my teachers—not so much from their lessons or the subject matter they tried to present, but from who they were as persons. So much of our growth and development is inflicted upon us by the psychological aberrations of the people we are forced to spend time with.

I do not remember with much kindness my first-grade teacher, Mrs. Olahan, who arrived at Wilson Avenue School the same year I did and who felt the need to assert her authority as soon as possible. Someone had told her in her education courses that discipline and control must first be established before education can take place. Unfortunately, I became the one upon whom that theory would be tested.

Early in October, Mrs. Olahan had the idea that it would be nice for her pupils to make Christmas gifts for their mothers. She asked us to bring in coffee cans which we proceeded to decorate and then wrap and give to our mothers during the Christmas break. I must have thought the idea utterly absurd. What was my mother going to do with a cut coffee can smeared with tempera paint that came off when you held it? This was another one of Olahan's lame-brained ideas, like the Father's Day gift of a fishing tackle box made from an egg carton. (She didn't know my father, or, for that matter, much about fishing.) So I refused to take the gift home.

Sometime in January, Olahan changed my seat. In a previous generation one moved to the head of the class as a reward for scholarship. Now the front seats were reserved for the incorrigible students that required the close supervision of the teacher. She kept her eye on me the entire time as I removed the contents of my desk and transferred it to the new location. The new student who took over my desk, the obnoxious and priggish Barbara Pearson, raised her hand: "Mrs. Olahan, there's an old coffee can in my desk."

"Young man, you come with me." She marched me down to the principal's office to tell Mrs. Yelton that I had failed to give my mother an empty coffee can for Christmas. I'm sure Mrs. Yelton had more important things to be concerned about, but it surprised me that I was being treated as a felon and that the coffee can incident was a major malfeasance of the elementary school law, right up there with such breaches of the social contract as chewing gum in class and forgetting your lunch money.

It was many years later when I became a teacher and had to deal with pregnant students in class, kids bringing guns and knives to school, glue-sniffers and crack addicts in the lavatories, and assaults on elderly teachers that I wished for the old days when the most serious thing a pupil could do was not give his mother a coffee can for Christmas.

There are some who will say that it was the erosion of discipline and respect in the schools and in the homes that led to the moral decay in America and to the increase in crime and drugs, the coming of the AIDS epidemic, and everything else that is wrong with our country. If it's not too late, I would like to offer an apology for starting it all with the coffee can.

# THE OAK IN INDEPENDENCE PARK

It was a green oasis in the middle of an urban landscape of crowded tenements and row homes, small stores and big warehouses. Independence Park in Newark's Ironbound section was a haven of quiet from the incessant traffic on the streets that surrounded the twelve and a half acres set aside by the city in 1896 for rest and recreation.

It was bordered on the south by Van Buren Street and East Side High School, great two-family dwellings and apartment buildings, and a few soda shops that served as hangouts for the students.

The hangouts for the adults were on the other side of the park, on Adams Street, where the East Side Social Club, the Broken Hearts Club, and St. George's Hall offered the mostly Italian men their own escape from their jobs and their wives. In reality, they were private gambling establishments where card games would continue into the late hours, and where all the local gossip could be found. You spent time here to try to make a few extra bucks at gin or five-card stud, or spend a few bucks on the latest merchandise that "fell off a truck." Speaking Italian helped, but was not required, although you were at a disadvantage if you didn't know all the swear words and hand gestures. St. George's Hall was the exception, however, but that was a church enterprise, and intended for Lithuanians who didn't know any swear words, or at least any that the Italians could pronounce.

To the west on Oliver Street was St. Michael's Russian Orthodox Church, adjacent to Our Lady of Mount Carmel Roman Catholic school and church. Mount Carmel was the national church of the Italians and the family church of my father. Although St. James was the territorial or parish church, many of the ethnic populations had their own churches with priests who could speak in the native tongue of their parishioners. The Germans went to St. Benedict's, around the block from where I lived. The Irish went to St. Aloysius, Poles to St. Casimir's, Portuguese to Our Lady of Fatima, Spanish to St. Joseph's, and the homeless to St. John's by the River. In the Newark patois, where words difficult to pronounce or remember were given their own accent or abbreviation, St. Benedict's became St. Bendix and the others St. Al's, St. Caz, Fat Lady, St. Joe's, and the bums's church.

Independence Park was aptly named. It gave me and my friends a sense of freedom from the confinement of the mean streets and crowded dwellings where we could unleash our boyish energies. Front lawns were non-existent in the city, and backyards were where you worked on cars, hung out laundry, or stored old appliances that might be needed for future parts. If you were fortunate, your grandfather might plant some tomatoes or zucchini or even a fig tree, although grape vines were not that uncommon.

It was the park, however, where we were free to roam. The ball fields were at the east end and the playground with sandboxes and jungle gyms at the other. The circular band platform in the middle of the park was not only the geographic center, but also the boundary for the older gangs that carefully guarded their particular turf. They didn't bother us younger kids, except to occasionally extort a "loan" from us.

The remainder of the park consisted of dense shrubbery, stately elms, oaks, sycamores, and occasional flower beds, which were the first to disappear to adorn the kitchen tables of nearby apartments. For us it was another world. This was Sherwood Forest from which we could launch our arrows at unsuspecting fat friars, the priests and seminarians from Mt. Carmel. This was the dense African jungle lair of Tarzan who would climb the massive trees and swing on ropes to terrify the packs of school girls, and where the older boys would lead them on safaris through the underbrush.

Sunday evening in the summer was Cowboy Night. This was when the bands and orchestras gave free concerts and the park was crowded with adults out for a pleasant evening. It was also when Independence Park became the Wild West and we loaded our water pistols at the numerous water fountains in order to ambush our prissy classmates who came to listen to music with their parents. Sometimes we would hide in the bushes near the band stage and aim our weapons up in the air so as to create an illusion of a possible shower, and delighted in the momentary look of concern on the faces of the band members.

# THE OAK IN INDEPENDENCE PARK

These were my Philistine days when I had little appreciation for music and the arts, but I was only eight or nine. In a few years I would find a new haven in the Newark Museum and the Metropolitan Museum of Art where culture would become my refuge, my alternative church and doorway to wonderful worlds of imagination and fantasy. When my world became more than I could handle, I would say with Blanche DuBois, "I don't want reality. I want magic."

I found magic in Independence Park, in my magic tree not far from the bocce courts where the old Italians rolled their heavy balls. My tree was the largest oak in the park, but you had to make your way through some entangled brush to find the path that led you there. I went to my oak often, sometimes to express gratitude and deliverance, but mostly to shed my tears and offer my desperate prayers. I brought to the oak the pain of my parents' troubled marriage, the fears of abandonment and loss, all the cuts and bruises of a child's warfare with the world. Here I brought the first feelings of love for a girl and the hurt of rejection. The oak knew all my emotions and felt the hormones and energy as it coursed through my body. As I leaned against its bark I could feel its strength and permanence infusing me with hope and the realization of life's transitory nature. I could hear it say to me, "I was here before you were born, and I will be here when you no longer have need of me."

No, I was not becoming a druid, though I might have considered it had I known what a druid was. My prayers and all my expressions of joy and fear, hope and despair, rage and doubt were directed to God. The oak was sacred ground. It was the place where, at that time in my life, I could sense the presence of God more acutely, and know that God knew who I was and where I was. The oak was my burning bush, out of which I heard God speak more clearly than any church or shrine.

In Celtic tradition, the natural world contains the presence of God. The Celts were not pantheists in that they believed in the deification of trees and stones, but panentheists who were able to discern the Creator in the works of creation, as one sees the artist in his or her art. Natural objects stored the energies and essences of their surroundings. Oak trees in particular were sacred to the religion of the Celtic tribes for they were the repository of tribal wisdom. The memory of trees retained all that was precious to their existence. To destroy a sacred oak was to cut the heart out of people who infused it with their life energy. It was to them what they wanted it to be.

# THE DWELLING PLACE OF WONDER

My oak was what I wanted it to be, what I needed it to be at that particular stage of my life. It offered me refuge and permanence in a world that was collapsing about me. Moses never returned to his holy bush. My oak is no longer a repository of memory, but a memory in my repository, and a cherished one at that.

I returned to Independence Park in recent years. The oak has long since been cut down. It served its purpose. Most of the trees and shrubs have been removed by the city. They had become places of concealment for muggers and drug dealers.

The world changes and time's everflowing stream bears all its sons away, but I am grateful for the islands in our lives on which we can be restored and renewed.

# THE MAGIC SANDBOX

EVEN FROM THE PERSPECTIVE of a child's-eye view, the sandbox in Independence Park was immense. An entire first-grade class could play in it without the need to assert territorial rights. It was a land of magic and imagination where castles were routine and battlegrounds for plastic soldiers were commonplace. It wasn't deep enough to tunnel through to China, but large enough to construct individual fortresses from behind which we could lob water balloons into enemy territory. That is, until Godzilla attacked wearing the shoes of eighth-graders from the nearby Catholic school. What did those nuns teach there that these kids would unleash all their nastiness on the smaller children as they delighted in running through our sand cities, destroying our castles and laying waste to our creativity?

It is the nature of some to build and the nature of others to destroy. In this sandbox we learned something about the impermanence of life. We built our houses and our mansions, our walls and bridges, our roads and tunnels, only to return the next day and see the entire infrastructure of our microcosmic world reduced to their primal state of an amorphous pile of sand.

Other kids would take our place later in the day and build their own civilizations on the ruins of what we had constructed, giving no thought to all our efforts and erasing all memory of what had preceded them. Their efforts as well would be superseded by the wind and the rain and rampaging footsteps of those engaged in their own play. It was one way in which we learned something about the transitory nature of life, that nothing we may do will have eternal permanence—at least in this world.

Some years later I would watch Tibetan monks construct a sand mandala, painstakingly applying grains of colored sand in the construction of

# THE DWELLING PLACE OF WONDER

an intricate design. Working in shifts, these monks would spend days to create a magnificent design. And when they were done they would sweep it all away and consign the sand to a swiftly moving stream. It was a dramatic lesson in the impermanence and futility of life, of how we can spend an entire lifetime doing what we think is important only to have it swept away by our own death and the passage of time. Shelley's "Ozymandias," king of kings, still lies in his desert where "the lone and level sands stretch far away."

But first-graders are existentialists. We didn't care about permanence. Our pleasure was in the doing, in the creating, in the playing, in the relationships with our classmates. We learned, not by what we did, but by how we did it and how we interacted with each other. Albert Camus was right in imagining Sisyphus happily pushing his boulder to the top of the hill only to see it roll down the other side. His joy was not in the accomplishment, but in the act of doing, in his own sense of being. Our worlds are made by what we imagine them to be.

One Saturday morning we were building a space station on one of the moons of Jupiter. Sherman, a childhood playmate for the day, held out his small hand containing a fistful of sand. "How many do you think there are?" he asked.

"What?"

"These little specks of sand?"

"Where?"

"In my hand? In this sandbox? In all the world? On all the planets? In all the universe?"

"Okay, Sherman, why don't you start counting and let me know what you come up with."

"Well, what if we measure how many pieces of sand there are in a teaspoon. And then we can see how many teaspoons there are in this pail, and then how many pails in this corner? If we keep multiplying we would eventually get an approximate number."

Sherman was smart, but this was stupid. "And what would you call this number?"

"Maybe we could think of something. Wouldn't it be great if we could number all of the atoms in the universe?"

"Yeah. Keep counting."

I think Sherman grew up to be a mathematician or an astrophysicist. I wonder how far he got with his counting.

# THE MAGIC SANDBOX

There was a short story by Arthur C. Clarke called "The Nine Billion Names of God," in which are Buddhists who believe that when all the possible names of God are written, the universe will end. They hire computer technicians who develop a program for listing the names of God, and when the computer spits out the final name, "overhead, without any fuss, the stars were going out," confirming the observation that there is a last time for everything. That was so evident in the sandbox.

There are times when the veil between fantasy and reality is blurred, when what you think you see is not necessarily what is; or, when you think about it years later, you wonder if it occurred in the physical world or in the world of your own making. Sanity is really a shared human delusion. To paraphrase that great linguistic philosopher Bill Clinton, what is, is, only when the majority agree that it is.

I was too young to engage in these verbal gymnastics, but I remember, or at least I think I remember, observing my life from a perspective of another person who came to me to offer suggestions as to what I should do. I was sitting on the edge of the sandbox contemplating my imaginary world when I saw a man in his twenties standing on the other side of the sandbox. He looked at me, somewhat puzzled, but with a degree of familiarity. I seemed to know him and he seemed to know me. I asked him, "Who are you?" He said, "I am you." Oh, no. Some college kid trying to play with my mind. "I am what you could be. I was who you are. We are the same person, but we chose different paths."

"I am who you may be." Are there parallel universes where we live different lives and every so often, whether in a dream or flash of recognition, we catch a glimpse of another self, or an aspect of ourselves?

It is said that when a person sees his *doppelganger*, his spiritual double, it is a sign of imminent exit from this life. However, sometimes it is a dimensional shift or a wrinkle in time. The German poet Johann Wolfgang von Goethe was riding on the road to Drusenheim in the eighteenth century when he saw his double riding toward him. His doppelganger was wearing a gray suit with gold trim. Eight years later, Goethe was again traveling on the same road, but in the opposite direction. He then realized he was wearing the very gray suit trimmed in gold that he had seen on his double eight years earlier! Had I been Goethe on that first encounter I think I might have stopped for a brief conversation.

But stranger, yet, some twenty years after the sandbox visitation, I had a dream in which I visited my past and saw a child playing in a sandbox. He stared at me and asked, "Who are you?" And I said, "I am you."

If I could visit my life as an observer to offer an occasional suggestion, would the course of my life be any different? How interesting—a self beside a self, or a self beyond a self. Isn't that the meaning of *paranoia*—mind beside or beyond itself?

Two men are having lunch in a restaurant when one ponders aloud, "Oh, to be eighteen again and know what I know now." The waitress, ready to take their order, says, "I'm eighteen. What do you know?"

It seems that all truth has to be discovered by oneself. There are many truths to be learned in life, but how those truths are appropriated and owned and applied are unique. I cannot even tell myself what it is to be. It must unfold as it should.

A notepad that I use for scribbling esoteric thoughts and disconnected ideas, the ravings of an eccentric mind or the gems of wisdom yet to be realized, bears the symbol of the United Church of Christ and its motto, "That they may all be one," which is based on the desire of Jesus in John's gospel "that they all may be one." Pope John Paul II, in his 1995 encyclical, *Ut unum sint*, sought to expand upon the Second Vatican Council's call for impassioned ecumenism among all Christians. The intent of Jesus, according to his vicar in Rome, was the unity of all Christians.

When I look at those words, I sometimes wonder if Jesus, or God speaking through him, really meant to include all people, not just those within the circles we draw. Buddhism has some insight here: all the lives that have ever been lived are but expressions of one great consciousness (God?), and collectively contribute to this universal mind.

The Apostle Paul writing to the Christians at Colossae expressed the hope that all things will be reconciled in the end under the sovereignty of Christ. Yet, there is something within me that doesn't agree with Clarke's scientists who say that there is an end to everything. There are no endings, only transitions. Perhaps the universe expands to infinity only to contract again, and that this expansion and contraction are occurring simultaneously. What appears to us to be the end may only be the beginning of God's new creation.

No life is ever lost or wasted, but fulfills the purpose of its existence. It may be only to affect the lives of others. Our world may become what we imagine it to be. We create our realities based upon our memories, perceptions, experiences. We see our world through ever-changing lenses, distorting it to conform to our prejudices and desires, but always, always growing in greater awareness of the wonder of being.

One could do worse than contemplate sand.

# A FRIEND FROM LITHUANIA

World War Two was a comic book war fought mostly in the pages of the books Dad had piled in the bathroom, or in films shown on the big screen at the Rivoli. It didn't hit home until a chubby kid named Marius showed up in Mrs. Wolverton's fourth-grade class. Marius was not a typical American name like Stevy, Billy, Joey, or Tommy. For him to fit in with our group, we would have had to add a "y" to his name, but it didn't seem right to call him "Mary," not after what he had been through.

Marius came from Lithuania. He had lived through the war and had been traumatized by it. He talked about the bombs and the fires. In Lithuania he had been afraid to go to bed at night and lived in constant fear of death from the skies. Now, in America, he was safe and secure—and grateful.

Marius's story did more for my sense of patriotism than anything I had read. The Pledge of Allegiance to the flag meant a lot more to me after hearing how he and his family escaped from the Nazis. It never occurred to me to ask who dropped the bombs on his city.

I liked Marius. He was self-confident, cultured, wise in the ways of the world. He had crammed a lot of living into his short span of years. We were only eight or nine years old, but Marius was going on twenty.

One Saturday he said to me, "Let's go to library." I thought he meant the Van Buren Street Branch Library, my favorite hang-out ever since Mrs. Olahan introduced us to this wonderful hall of books on a second-grade field trip.

"No," said Marius, "we go to big library uptown."

The main library on Washington Street was a bus ride away, in the cultural center of Newark. In those days, Newark did indeed have a cultural

# A FRIEND FROM LITHUANIA

center. The Newark Museum was a few doors away on the other side of the prestigious Second Presbyterian Church. The museum, library, church, along with the Ballantine Mansion, all fronted Washington Park with its massive statue of the general in front of his horse.

I never paid much attention to Newark's monuments, but there were several that were impressive. Gutzon Borglum, the Scandinavian sculptor who carved Mount Rushmore, had a number of statues in Newark. The seated Lincoln with his stovepipe hat on the bench next to him was in front of the Essex County courthouse. Many photos were taken of people sitting next to Mr. Lincoln, the precursor of the cardboard cut-out president. There was also a statue of "The Indian and the Puritan" near the library. Borglum's largest and most formidable work was the massive "Wars of America" in Military Park. It was so big that it even had a door in the back. A stranger sitting on a park bench told me that was where they buried Newark's war dead.

There was also a statue of Seth Boyden standing alongside an anvil. I often wondered why they would erect a statue to a blacksmith. Later I learned that he was an industrialist who made malleable iron, built locomotives, improved the process of making patent leather, invented a hatmaking machine, built a fire engine, and created the finest strawberries—all hammered out on his anvil, I suppose. Boyden, like fellow New Jersey inventor Thomas Edison, could never stay focused. Once he invented something, he would move on to other endeavors. At least Edison had the good sense to profit by his work. But I liked the fact that he could think of so many things all at once—and probably before breakfast.

Museums and libraries seemed to be constructed like ancient temples dedicated to the gods and goddesses of learning and the arts. Of course, the name "museum" comes from the Muses, those nine young ladies eternally playing their instruments, dancing, singing, doing all those creative things. These twentieth-century buildings were to perpetuate their work for all time—an Akashic record of human achievement that would exist for all time, or at least until some future despot decided it wasn't necessary since God knows all that stuff already. Didn't Caliph Omar administer the *coup de gras* to the great library at Alexandria in 641 saying that anything worth knowing was already in the Koran, and if it wasn't in the Koran, it wasn't necessary? He then proceeded to stuff the volumes that had escaped destruction by Julius Caesar and later by Christian fanatics into the bakery ovens of his Arab army and the bathhouses of Alexandria. Thus passes the memory of humankind and all that was regarded as eternal truth.

The Newark Public Library was constructed in 1903 in an Italian Renaissance design and was meant to look imposing. It was also intimidating. It not only said, "This is important," it also said "Kids Keep Out!" At least the Newark Museum had a back entrance for kids to sneak into the children's section, but the library had this immense entrance hall with big desks and people in uniforms who looked into women's purses and shopping bags. There were also little rooms off to the side. I asked Marius if that was where they did the strip searches of persons they suspected of smuggling out books. "No," he said, "those doors lead down to the cells where they lock up people for bringing in overdue books and who can't pay the fine."

We discovered other cells, glass enclosed cubicles where we could listen to classical music on large, but very fragile, records that ran at 78 rpm. They were kept in big albums that the attendant wouldn't let us handle, but was willing to play for us. Marius reveled in the scratchy sounds, but at that age I found culture boring. We were worlds apart.

Once I became accustomed to it, the library was fun. It opened up to me so many other worlds that didn't exist in the asphalt environment of a noisy and polluted city. I could live in Sherwood Forest with Robin and Little John or ride with Zorro in old California. I enjoyed Greek and Roman mythology best. Sometimes I would pretend that the book stacks were Minos's labyrinth. We would run through the stacks in search of Ariadne until the assistant librarian would grab us. The Minotaur would then escort us from fantasy to reality, an unfriendly Virgil guiding us from Paradise.

The library helped me see the world as I would have liked it to be. Daydreams are not only useful in preserving one's mental health, but necessary for the ordering of reality. Each person creates his or her own reality, the world in which one lives. Our shared reality is what we consider normality. If a person insists on maintaining his reality that the rest of us consider too bizarre, we sometimes institutionalize him. Sanity is what a majority of people agree it is.

Nevertheless, the library provided me with open windows to see life as it could be, and sometimes as it could never be. Life was learning to sort through the differences. Though I have learned to focus on what is needful, healing, and helpful, there are many times when I would like to cut the mind's tether and soar to other dimensions.

## A FRIEND FROM LITHUANIA

The books with which I once surrounded myself were seeds planted years ago and are still bearing fruit.

I grew up in a Newark that was violent, dirty, overpopulated, segregated, and dangerous. I also grew up in a city of art and culture, of beautiful parks and pools, of friendly people who wanted to be kind and helpful, of old world charm and ways and traditions that were rapidly becoming extinct. It was all there. It depended upon what you wanted to see and what you closed your eyes to. Unfortunately, too many of Newark's residents closed their eyes to what was happening in their city. Others, myself included, left the city for college or jobs or retirement and never came back. Newark in the sixties went through a violent transition of death and rebirth, but it is now becoming the city I dreamed about.

Whether it becomes an alabaster city undimmed by human tears remains to be seen. It certainly had enough of tears—I left a few behind myself. Now, when I drive by on the turnpike, I see the city gleaming in the distance in the soft glow of twilight, and I think that it is the long view that obscures the decadence and decay, the worm holes of a hundred thousand lives that have gnawed away at what our Puritan forebears had left us. However, like Eurydice, one returns to hell when one looks back to the past with too much yearning, or, like Lot's wife, becomes a pillar of salt transfixed in time because she would not face her future. No life should be judged by one or two events or by where one has come from. We are all in a state of becoming. That is true for cities as well as people.

# CIRCUMAMBULATING THE MARNE

WORLD WAR II WAS not as graphic nor as violent for children living in the States—not the way Vietnam was to be, with its daily body counts and helicopter assaults depicted on the evening news. We learned of the Big War mostly through its effect upon the adults in our lives and their conversations.

Mom had a job with Northern Feather Works making sleeping bags for the GIs. She and her co-workers, to relieve the boredom and make life more interesting for soldiers getting ready to go to war, would write bits of poetry and notes and pin them inside the bags. One day a government inspector appeared and assembled the workforce. He wanted to know who was putting the notes in the sleeping bags. Not one of the girls spoke up. Then, with a big grin on his face, the inspector, who was called "Tex," said, "Well, I want you all to keep it up. It's good for morale and the guys appreciate what you are doing."

My mother was always a prolific letter writer. I never got a postcard from her that wasn't covered with words. She wrote to everyone. Before the war she would write to a kid from the neighborhood that they called "Hot Dogs." He was a sailor on one of the ships that was at Pearl Harbor on that infamous Sunday morning in 1941. He was just a high school friend, but Mom's endearing letters spoke of love and home and those sentiments a sailor would die for.

Hot Dogs was in love with this blonde teenager from Marne Street and wanted to leave the Navy and come home to her, but her father, Lucas, said she was too young to get married. Heartbroken, he remained in the Navy;

but he kept the letters, and they ended up entombed at the bottom of Pearl Harbor.

I imagine those letters somehow floating to the surface and ending up on a Hawaiian beach somewhere where another young girl would read them and reconstruct the context in her imagination. What a Hollywood screenplay that would make—letters from the past breaking free from a watery grave to haunt the lives of those grown old and who have moved in other directions. We are always influenced by the past, and many times it is not even our own past. It seems that life has no intrinsic meaning, and life is only how we interpret it. As one postmodern philosopher observed, it's all hermeneutics. The meaning of events depends upon the context in which they occur.

World War II had little meaning for five-year-olds. After the war we heard all the stories of armies and invasions—of many deaths, both military and civilian . We heard the names of places we could hardly pronounce and had no idea where they were. The Battle of Britain—"their finest hour"—was recreated by throwing balsa cutouts of planes into the air and shooting them down with rubber bands. The cliffs of Normandy were assaulted by climbing over the back of the sofa and fighting through a maze of chair legs under the dining room table. But the war would soon be forgotten. Children had more important things to do than fight evil and save the world. That would be simply a by-product of growing up.

Uncle Frank Rygiel, Dottie's husband, was with the Army Rangers in the South Pacific. I didn't hear much about him until after the war when family gatherings were occasions to hear of his exploits. He was a reluctant storyteller, but we knew we could get him going on Sunday afternoons when "Victory at Sea" was on. We would ask him, "Is that true? Is that the way it really was?" And he would tell us.

Marne Street on a summer's evening was like Vienna's famed Ring Strasse—a place to see and be seen. Neighbors would take turns visiting with one another. There was a certain ritual that was observed after supper. Supper was always the Sunday evening meal served at six. The rest of the week it was called dinner (dinner on Sundays was the noon meal). It didn't matter what you served or how formal it was, these were always the designations and added a touch of class to an immigrant household where we would frequently dine on chicken soup and buttered toast, and of course Natalie's *pièce de résistance*, fruit-flavored gelatin with embedded bananas.

After this magnificent repast we would sit on the front stoop and greet the passersby.

Some would offer a "Hello, how are you?" as they passed on down the street. Some would pause for a moment or two, and others, after the perfunctory comments about the weather, would discuss the latest gossip, which usually involved neighbors, church, jobs, and Mr. Truman—usually in that order of priority.

At some point, when the traffic seemed to slow, Lucas would say that it was now our turn, and we would begin our circumambulation of the block. We, too, would stop and talk with neighbors about matters that were probably of great importance at the time but were terribly boring to me.

I would always hope to be lucky enough when Rudy the Bootlegger came home. Rudy drove a big, black sedan that was unmistakable. When he pulled up to his house on Marne Street the neighborhood kids would run to greet him. Rudy had a habit of throwing his pocket change in the street and delighted in watching the mad scramble for the coins. I think he kept them just for that occasion. I had also heard that John D. Rockefeller did the same, but Rockefeller only threw dimes (cheapskate).

If Rudy was home during the week, he would watch for the produce peddler in his horse-drawn wagon. The peddler would stop in front of Rudy's house and Rudy would buy the entire contents from the farmer and then invite all the housewives to come with their bags and help themselves.

Prohibition had ended more than a decade before, but old habits die hard, and Rudy still continued to make his mash in the basement. His neighborly largesse only served to insure that his activities remained clandestine. He was found a few years later in his bathtub, drowned in his own liquor. It wasn't quite the butt of malmsey into which the Duke of Clarence was thrown by Richard III, but it seemed appropriate.

Walking with Lucas could be interesting, but it could also be frightfully boring. The times have changed, but the issues were the same: shop talk, politics, neighborhood gossip, what the pastor said that morning, and of course predictions of the coming week's weather.

My reward for enduring these Sunday evening peripatetics was a stop at Dolly's on Niagara Street for ice cream. The ice cream of memory is always more delicious and flavorful than the reality, and I would often think of those double-dip sugar cones wrapped in wax paper. The anticipation of the first lick magnified the pleasure of the experience. I endured the walks around the block and groaned at every stop, but after watching the jerk behind the counter dip into the five-gallon tub of chocolate and extract a bit of heaven, the reward was well worth it. (How the meanings of words can change in a generation—the "soda jerk" was so-called because he would "jerk" the handle on the soda-dispenser after pumping flavored syrup in a glass.) I had to wait until we returned home so that we could eat our cones together. An ancillary benefit of postponing our joy was that we no longer had to stop and talk to any more neighbors. Lucas would end any interruption on our homeward journey with "have to get home before the ice cream melts."

Whenever I was impatient—and it was often—Natalie would say, "You have to wait for heaven." The implication, of course, was that you had to put up with a lot of hell first. Enduring the bad parts of life somehow were supposed to make the good parts more pleasurable. I suppose that this is true, but when it comes to ice cream, I am still impatient. When I bring home a quart of ice cream, I always take a spoonful before putting it in the freezer. "Quality control," I would tell the kids. They, of course, maintain that I have never met a quart of ice cream I didn't like.

Marne Street was idyllic. Toward the end of the nineteenth century a developer bought large tracts of land bordering the Newark marshes and laid them out with neat squares and built tiny four-room two-story houses with just enough ground in the back for a small garden or a pigeon or a chicken coop. What made the streets so wonderful was the scarcity of automobiles and the abundance of huge elms and oaks and maples that lined the sidewalks providing a leafy canopy above the street. On a quiet Sunday afternoon, as I waited for the soft-pretzel man to come in his horse-drawn wagon, I would be entertained by the streams of sunlight breaking through the branches and splotching the shadows with dazzlements. It could have been a small nineteenth century village scene, but it was Newark in the late forties, a time reluctant to surrender its past to the future. Innocence passed all too quickly.

My uncle, Richard Wertz, had been a deep-sea diver and had also attended the Casey Jones School of Aeronautics in California. When he came home from the Navy, he took up residence in the temporary barracks set up in Weequahic Park—a kind of half-way encampment before re-entering the civilian world. After he had moved to the third-floor apartment in Luigi Serio's house, he would drive us to Weequahic Park to see if any of his shipmates were still there. They weren't, but I was impressed at how quickly they had erected those buildings and a little annoyed at what they had done to the park. It was a time of transition. But then, every time is a time of transition. There is no present moment, but simply change from past to future, and it was increasingly hard to hold on to that past.

Dad also tried his luck with the Navy. When the war broke out, he enlisted. His friends gave him quite a send-off—big party, gifts, money, watch, cards, mementos. Two weeks after he left for boot camp, Mom heard an intruder climbing in through the bedroom window. Dad was returning from his hitch with the Navy. Too many blows to the head in his boxing career had caused him to black out, so the Navy sent him home. Since he went off without a key to the house and came back in the middle of the night, he decided to make his surreptitious entry. Typically, he never returned any of his going-away gifts.

# HOLOCAUST

THE HORRORS OF WAR were not suitable dinner conversation, especially when small children were present. It was nevertheless hard to avoid. We all knew relatives and friends of relatives who had answered their country's call, but children were spared the details of death and destruction.

Hell intruded our lives in momentary revelations. The first epiphany of evil of cosmic proportion was a cool spring day early in May 1945. The surrender of Germany was imminent. The newspapers were talking about the liberation of the death camps and how many Jews had died in the massive slaughter. At that age I didn't know what a Jew was, and the term "holocaust" had not yet entered my vocabulary.

Later that year Aunt Elsie said that Hitler had been killing the Jews—millions of them. How many was a million? The number didn't mean much. But if I knew one Jew, then that would mean something. Elsie said that Arlene was Jewish.

Arlene was a little girl four years older than I who lived around the block. In a child's microcosm it could have been another country. Arlene was beautiful, a sweet and pleasant girl. I would see her often walking home from school and she would always stop and say hello. Arlene was an icon of innocence who in my memory I would always picture as Anne Frank—bright, articulate, and vulnerable—someone who needed protection. As the only Jew that I had known at that time (and I didn't really know it until Elsie's revelation), I would have nightmares of her as a victim of the gas ovens at Auschwitz. It was a telling moment when all the world seemed so unsafe and treacherous. It remained a constant and haunting memory even after Arlene graduated as valedictorian of her high school class.

# THE DWELLING PLACE OF WONDER

For the most part, though, the war would soon be over and become a distant memory. Children could now focus on other things and use their imaginations in more peaceful pursuits. The horrors of war and annihilation would become a footnote in the process of growing up. I was to learn otherwise.

I never paid much attention to the books on the shelf in my grandparent's living room. The house was very small, only four rooms and a basement kitchen. The living room consisted of a sofa, two chairs, a table with a radio—our connection to the world—and a bookcase. The prominence of these five shelves indicated that this was something important, almost sacred. But this was a time when I was just learning to read, and the books, which belonged to Elsie, did not have enough pictures to entertain my young mind while I struggled with deciphering the words.

Some of the books did have pictures: Seversky's *Victory Through Air Power*, with its neat photos of post-World War I aircraft; and *Green Mansions*, by W. H. Hudson, with its mysterious, haunting images of the young girl Rima blending into the darkness of the Amazon rainforest.

There were books without pictures that I ignored, but I remember their titles and would read some of them later: *Random Harvest, Look Homeward Angel, Gone With the Wind, Colonel Effingham's Raid, Cross Creek,* and others.

Elsie read a lot and must have been right-brain dominant. Her artist soul led her on journeys through literature, art, music, movies, museums, and the popular mystery bus trips, who like the patriarch Abraham "went out, not knowing where he was to go." Elsie loved the excitement and discovery of something new, whether a Victorian village in Cape May or Newark's reservoir at Wanaque.

Whatever Elsie did, she preserved. Her life, and that of the family, was documented in thousands of snapshots. Whatever she read, she kept. The Elsie Wertz method of housekeeping was legendary. She would empty the contents of her room to decide what was to be thrown out, and finding that there was too much that she wanted to keep, she would return her clutter to its original state.

One book that Elsie did not keep in the bookcase, but rather on a shelf in her closet was a massive volume of Currier and Ives prints, luxuriously bound in white leather. Occasionally she would permit me to leaf through this visionary experience of a world that existed before I did. It was good escapism and filled my need for fantasy and nostalgia. Nostalgia has always been a longing for a time in which I never lived, but wished so hard that I had that it made me feel as though I did.

Through these old prints I could experience the 1870's, visit Central Park on clear, crisp day to see the lake covered with skaters, or travel to the West and see a herd of buffalo stop a locomotive. There were glimpses of trout fisherman in northern streams, idyllic plantation life in the antebellum South, the grandeur of the Rockies, the strength and anger of an ocean storm vented against a lone vessel.

It never occurred to me at the time how our worldview is distorted by the words and images that surround us in our formative years. The one picture I avoided in Currier and Ives was entitled "The Bad Man at the Hour of Death." The skeleton pointing his spear at the cowering man in his bedsheet reminded me of how close we are to death at any moment of our lives.

There was another book on my grandmother's shelf: *Mein Kampf,* by Adolf Hitler. I was puzzled why a book by this arch-demon would be in my grandparents' possession. The enemies of the state had been depicted in posters and in speech as personifications of evil. Even caricatures of Hitler and Tojo represented them as mad-eyed lunatics bent on killing. Why would Hitler's book be on our shelf?

It wasn't until many years later that I began to understand what was in the minds of the German-American community in Newark while I was growing up. I had just become the pastor of St. John's United Church of Christ in Kutztown, Pennsylvania—a church that had deep German roots going back to the early eighteenth century. These Germans, however, were German only in their ethnicity and held no sympathies during the war for the country of their ancestry. But, being Germanic in culture, the Pennsylvania German congregations often attracted more recent immigrants to this country.

During my first week in Kutztown I received a phone call from one of these twentieth-century immigrants who had married a member of my new congregation. Guenther Driemel had heard that I had grown up in Newark and was ordained in St. Stephan's Church. When Guenther arrived in this country, he, too, had gone to St. Stephan's. After some conversation about mutual acquaintances from our pasts, Guenther said that St. Stephan's had many members who were associated with the German-American Bund. I knew that the Bund had been active in Newark in the thirties and had some run-ins with the sizeable Jewish community. That had surprised me since Newark had a Jewish mayor, Meyer Ellenstein, in the year I was born.

In discussing this dark side of my city's past, and probably that of my church, and wondering why *Mein Kampf* would be in our home, I learned that the proud Germans had been so demoralized by their defeat in the First World War that they were looking for anyone and anything that would restore their sense of self-pride. The Nationalist Socialist German Workers Party offered the opportunity for Germans to once again feel good about themselves. However, as we have seen so many times in history, good intentions can escalate into a distortion of its original purpose, and extremism can begin the slow descent into hell. Barry Goldwater sought to remind us that "extremism in the defense of liberty is no vice," and that "moderation in the pursuit of justice is no virtue," but unchecked extremism without responsibility and without respect for the liberties of others can only lead to perdition and the loss of one's soul.

To their credit, most of these German-Americans in Newark eventually saw through the evil that was being perpetrated upon the world and renounced any connection with the Bund. The honor roll at St. Stephan's was long with the names of those who served their country to rid the world of this horror.

I was seven or eight years old when I arrived at school one morning to learn that one of my classmates had been killed in a vacant lot at Avenue L and Backus Streets. The newspapers at that time did not use words like "raped" or "sexually molested." Certainly children would not understand what that meant, and in a sexually repressed age such matters were seldom discussed. All that it meant to us was that our friend and classmate was no longer with us and that some evil person had taken her life. Seeing her lying in her coffin in the Bibbo Funeral Home was my first real encounter with a dead person, and I thought of that skeleton in the Currier and Ives print. The words of Gene Autry's country-western song became relevant: "She was only seven when she was called to heaven. That little kid sister of mine." I could not get the words out of my head.

The thought of Arlene being gassed. Hitler killing the Jews. Death stalking both the evil and the innocent. *Mein Kampf* in our living room. In the midst of life we are in death. The skeleton intrudes upon us and reminds even little kids that life in this world is not forever. When you are seven or

# HOLOCAUST

eight or eighteen you are immortal. Death has little meaning even when he comes into your life and walks beside you.

In the fifties, many survivors of the Holocaust came to New Jersey, often settling with families in the Weequahic section. I never really met any of them until working a summer job at Liquid Carbonic, a manufacturer of dry ice and carbon dioxide in Belleville. There was a thin, gaunt Polish Jew who also worked there. He had deep-set haunting eyes, but wore a continual smile. He spoke little English and was very frugal with the words he did know. I thought it odd that he wore long-sleeved shirts even on the hottest days of August. In a union shop where employees sought creative ways to avoid doing their work, this man went about his job without complaint and without taking the required twenty-minute coffee breaks twice a day.

Once, while reaching for a lever, his arm extended beyond his shirt cuff and then I understood the reason for his long sleeves. On his forearm was tattooed a number. It could only mean one thing: his Nazi captors had marked him for death, but he had survived. I thought of the irony that he was now working at Liquid Carbonic filling cylinders with gas.

While this Polish Jew was embarrassed by his captivity, perhaps that he had survived while so many of his faith had not, and therefore he sought to conceal his identity as a victim, Harry the tailor was not.

Harry lived in a third floor apartment with his wife in Bloomfield. My brother Bob knew him, and as Bob began to lose weight from his illness, he would take his suits to Harry for alteration. We never knew Harry's full name and probably never bothered to ask. He was always Harry the Tailor, and later simply Harry Taylor.

Harry was a Holocaust survivor and he was not ashamed to talk about it. Whenever we visited his apartment he always had the news on or some political talk show. He made the point that one must always be involved in politics. It is when you don't care what kind of government you have that you get the government you deserve. He referred to Germany and made his point.

I asked him how he managed to survive and his answer was simple: he had a trade that the Nazis found useful. They had no need for teachers, artists, or philosophers, but tailors they could use. When you were dispensable, you were dispensed with.

A few years later I found myself in Jerusalem working at the City of David archaeological project through the Hebrew University. No one

# THE DWELLING PLACE OF WONDER

should go to Jerusalem without visiting Yad Vashem, the memorial to the victims of the Holocaust. Unlike the soaring cathedrals of Europe erected to the glory of God as monuments to the grandeur of human art and creativity, here is a shrine to the unspeakable terrors wrought by the dark side of the human spirit.

The eerie silence of the stark stones and hushed voices of visitors cannot mask the whispers of the dead—more than six million souls—whose only message is "Do not forget." Here in the pavement beneath the Ner Tamid, the eternal light of the presence of God, are the names of the camps—Berkenau, Auschwitz, Dachau, Treblinka. You walk with careful steps, for you walk among the unsilent dead.

This is the Hall of Remembrance, where in addition to the names of all twenty-two "killing" camps there is a black mosaic floor made up of six million tiny tiles, one for every Jew that died; and although the individual tiles are very small, the floor covers a large area. One is impressed with how vast a number six million is. One also realizes how efficient human beings can be at killing one another. Buried beneath an eternal flame lie human ashes taken from each one of those camps, and one can almost hear the faint echo of W. B. Yeat's words, "tread softly because you tread on my dreams"—dreams unfulfilled and hopes unrealized.

But perhaps the most moving memorial of all is the Children's Memorial. One and a half million children were killed in the Holocaust, and every single one of them is remembered daily by name. You file into a circular, darkened room, with just a handrail around the wall to guide you. The center of the room is made up of a large glass pillar, which has five candles inside it. But there are also numerous mirrors at different angles inside the pillar, so that the flames from the five candles are reflected about a million and a half times. As you look up or down or through the pillar, all you can see is flickering candle flames, like so many stars in an eternal night. And at the same time, a continuous commentary reads out the names of the children who died—"Martin Goldstein, aged six years, Holland; Ruth Schenkel aged 13 years, Germany"—and so on. Few people emerge from the Children's Memorial with dry eyes.

The Hall of Memories is enough to tear one's soul apart at the thought of such cosmic evil let loose in the world. Joseph Stalin is reputed to have said, "A single death is a tragedy; a million deaths is a statistic." It is almost impossible to comprehend the magnitude and meaning of millions of deaths. "Unto every person there is a name," is a project to give identity

# HOLOCAUST

and remembrance to each of the more than six million lives destroyed. In personalizing each individual, one can move from statistic to tragedy. The Hall of Names recognizes that God has created each person as a unique individual with his or her own purpose in the life of the universe.

How can one forgive such a horror? How does one even seek forgiveness?

Johann tried. Johann was a German school teacher who I met while staying at Christ Church Hospice in Jerusalem. The Church of England hospice was just inside Jaffa Gate in the Old City and had attracted guests from all over Europe and North America. Some were there as tourists, some on business or on pilgrimage. Some were there because they felt they had to be in Jerusalem.

Johann was a baptized Lutheran in Jerusalem studying to become a rabbi. I asked him why he had converted to Judaism. He said that his father and mother had lived through the German nightmare as good and loyal Germans devoted to their country. They knew nothing of what was happening to the Jews—or didn't want to know. There were some, he said, that at the end of the war, when the realization set in of the magnitude of Hitler's megalomania, it created such anguish in these good Christians that they could not bear the guilt and remorse. Many committed suicide because of their depression and profound sense of guilt. It was understandable that the Nazi war criminals would take their own lives to avoid execution, but for simple German citizens who did nothing to be driven to this end was an indication of how devastating was the revelation.

But that was precisely the point. Their guilt was that they did nothing; they sought to know nothing, and by their silence were complicit in this horror. However, many of these good Germans had progressed from *apatheia* to *psychalgia,* where they were feeling physically what they had felt in their souls.

Some, of course, still refused to believe what had happened in the death camps, or just wanted to ignore it. When I asked our German tour guide to take us to Dachau, he asked, "Why would you want to go there? It's too depressing."

Johann was in Israel to atone for the Holocaust by becoming a Jew. He felt that the only way to experience the pain and suffering of the Holocaust victims was to become a Jew himself. One must walk in the shoes of the persecuted, he said. It was like God becoming human in Jesus Christ in order to experience the pain, suffering, and death of the crucifixion. Without getting into a protracted discussion of patripassianism, I simply accepted Johann's need for expiation and wished him well in finding peace for his soul.

Are there crimes so heinous that even God cannot forgive? One can imagine Jesus welcoming Judas to the messianic banquet and offering the cup of forgiveness. But how do you do this after so many deaths? Simon Wiesenthal, who had eighty-nine of his relatives murdered by the Nazis, could not offer absolution to the wounded German soldier who sought his forgiveness. He left the man to his own torment.

Many years ago I heard a story told by a Presbyterian pastor named Ernie, who ministered to a rather unique congregation in Newark, New Jersey. This congregation consisted mostly of Jews who had converted to Christianity, many because of Ernie. I had forgotten about this story until being reminded of it by a ministerial colleague a few years ago. I have been trying to track down its source in print. It is so poignant and descriptive of how the Holocaust affects us even after more than half a century.

Ernie grew up in Holland, and when the war came and the Gestapo were rounding up the Jews, Ernie went into hiding. Like Anne Frank, he was concealed by a Christian family. But one day in 1944 there was a knock on the door and the Gestapo took both the Jews and the Christians. They were sent to the concentration camp at Theresienstadt.

When they arrived at the camp, they were divided into two lines. Ernie survived because he was young and strong. He was put to work pushing the victims, mostly women and children, into the gas chamber. For almost a year he worked in the death camp. His hate kept him alive. And then one day in the spring of 1945 he woke up and found the camp empty of German guards. Thinking it was a trick, the Jews lined up for roll call and stood in the yard until noon. Then the Americans came, and from that day on Ernie equated Savior with American.

After the liberation, Ernie returned to Holland and learned that his entire family had been exterminated, and also the family with whom he stayed, the family that had given him shelter. There was only one survivor—the daughter. He married her and became a Christian and emigrated to the United States.

The story, however, doesn't end there. Ernie decided to go into the ministry. Perhaps he felt he had to pay back what he owed to this Christian family who had given their lives for him. Not unlike Johann.

# HOLOCAUST

Ernie went to seminary. He had a class that was a problem for him. He had grown to hate Germans with a hatred that tore at his very soul. It wasn't just the Nazis; he became physically sick when he was in the presence of anyone who looked German. He not only hated Germans, but the German language, the German culture. And now he found himself in a class that was taught by a German professor.

After sitting in that class for several sessions, his hatred seething in him, destroying his concentration, and conflicting with the Christian ethic of love and forgiveness, he could take it no longer. He decided to confront the professor.

He went to his office and poured out his soul. He hated the Germans. He could not forgive them for killing his family, for forcing him to kill his own people by pushing them into the gas chamber. He then rolled up his sleeve and showed the professor the tattooed number that marked him as a prisoner.

At first the professor said nothing. He walked to the window and stared into the silence for a long time. With his face still turned away, the professor spoke slowly. He, too, had a problem with forgiveness. He had recognized Ernie when he entered his class, and he had hatred for his student. He said that he, too, had been a prisoner of the Nazis—in fact, in the same prison camp. He rolled up his sleeve and there was the tattooed number on his wrist. How could he forgive this man who stood before him, this man whom he had seen push his wife into the gas chamber?

We are all guilty. We all dwell in the darkness at some point in our lives. We all stand in need of the grace of God. None of us deserves God's grace, and we certainly could not withstand God's justice. But to break the cycle of hatred and violence, frustration and despair, tragedy and sorrow, we must be dispensers of the love of God, and that begins by remembering who we are as humans and what we are capable of becoming.

Arlene standing before me in her black woolen coat and babushka with the face of innocence has become an iconic image of those who did not survive the greatest horror of our generation.

# THE CRONE

The small country shack with a wood shingle roof, weathered clapboard sides, and a stovepipe extending through the roof was appropriate for the back hills of West Virginia, but this was a city lot in Newark, New Jersey, across from our house on Marne Street.

The old woman who lived there was reclusive. Her three-room house sat back from the street, and the front yard was always overgrown and entangled with weeds and decaying vegetation. Edgar Allen Poe would have been inspired by the setting.

We seldom caught sight of this mysterious crone. Occasionally she would make an appearance in the yard, inviting stares from passersby who had the morbid curiosity associated with being confronted by the dead (or those who ought to be). The Italian women in the neighborhood would make the sign of the horns, or *manu cornuto*, and whisper "*maloic scata*," an expression in Southern Italian dialect for warding off the evil eye. She seemed always to be dressed in black, the so-called "widow's weeds" of an earlier time or a different culture. Both her dress and black apron were in tatters. Her face was as weathered as her house and gnarled almost to the point of distortion, keeping her mouth in a perpetual half-smile that also revealed her missing teeth. When she spoke, and it was seldom, it was in a high-pitched voice that crackled like flame on dried kindling. There was just a hint of an accent—Eastern European possibly. No one knew.

We never saw her leave her house and yard, and seldom saw anyone enter. This, of course, only embellished the stories that were going around. The kids in the neighborhood would speak of secret passageways and nightly excursions to forage for food. The rattling of a trash can in the alley would prompt the observation that the old woman was hunting her dinner.

# THE CRONE

If we didn't see one of our friends for a while, someone would say that she was dining well that night, and wonder how long the leftovers would last.

For the most part, the old woman was ignored by the neighbors—except at Halloween. An old crone in a dimly lit, ramshackle house conjured fantasies of ghosts and hauntings and witchcraft. No one would take the dare to knock on her door. We had all heard about Hansel and Gretel. Taunts were made at a safe distance, but for the most part she was much too frightening to approach.

Once, in Sunday School, we discussed the story of the Good Samaritan and what it meant to be a good neighbor. We talked about showing kindness to the stranger and to those we don't know, especially when it is done in secret.

I didn't put my quarter in the offering plate that Sunday. Instead, on the way home from church I stopped at Schrotts' Bakery and bought a loaf of freshly baked bread. With a lot of trepidation, I undid the latch on the gate and walked up to the crone's house and set the white bag on her doorstep. There was no doorbell so I rapped softly and then ran like hell.

I could see her house from the front window of our apartment. She didn't answer my knock, but by evening the bread was gone. I don't remember whether I hoped she had seen me do what I thought was a good deed, or was wishing she didn't know, making the gift from an anonymous person seem more valued. Perhaps, whether she had seen it or not, she could have been suspicious of an unexpected gift from a stranger. I suppose in this day she would have summoned the bomb squad.

How much is communicated in a gift? What is in the heart of the giver? What is in the mind of the receiver? What does the gift itself say?

The sharing of bread is seen by the church as an act of communion, but the Apostle Paul suggests that it is only communion when Christ is discerned as spiritually present. Was this an act of communion or an incomplete sacrament? Where was the spiritual link of her soul with mine? We did not, each of us, know the Christ in the breaking of the bread. There was no reconciliation in this hit-and-run communion.

But it was a redemptive act—at least for me. The old woman died sometime later that month. Coming home from school I saw the ambulance in the street. They carried her out on a litter; she was covered from head to foot. Only part of her hand could be seen where the white sheet was pushed back a little. On her withered, arthritic finger was a gold wedding band.

# THE DWELLING PLACE OF WONDER

I have thought about that ring of gold and the loaf of bread. Who was this strange woman who lived on my street for so many years? I never knew her name or where she had come from. Who was her husband? Did they have any children? What were her hopes and dreams before they came to dust in this run-down house in a busy city? What wisdom did she possess that she could not communicate that died with her? How much we lose when we fail to know and to love the strangers who live around us.

We really are as ships that pass in the night, distant lights on a vast horizon. We note one another's presence in the world, but we seldom know what illuminates the interior of another's soul. But even in a brief passage, without a word exchanged, we can become changed forever.

I am convinced that nothing is ever lost. All the particles of our existence, the lost fragments of events, the broken shards of our lives, and all the people we have ever known come together as flecks of paint on the huge canvas of eternal existence and add to the complex picture of who we are, and how we fit into the even greater picture of God's design.

Somewhere, sometime in the distant hereafter I will meet the old woman and we will know each other by the loaf of bread at her doorstep.

# BANANA BOB SLEEPS WITH THE FISHES

The names were colorful enough—Ray Rats, Cigarface, Plywood, Stash—but the exploits of these characters were even more so. Banana Bob got his name from running merchant ships to South America carrying cargoes of bananas. So he said; the guys on the dock preferred a more crass etymology. Bob had been in the Navy during the Second World War and saw action in the Pacific. All he ever talked about was sex and sea. Everyone knew about his ability to land a big fish or a buxom broad, including his wife Carla. She tolerated his cheating heart for the sake of the children, but she let him know how she felt about it.

Bob always said that he wanted to be buried at sea when the time came. He wanted his spirit to be able to roam the depths of the ocean and travel the sea lanes to the farthest reaches of the earth. He definitely didn't want to be confined to a box planted in a plot of ground. He was only forty-eight when I knew him, and his death wouldn't come for a good many years. He enjoyed life and all its pleasures. His idea of heaven was a few cases of beer, a sunny day on a fishing boat trolling for blues off Atlantic Highlands with a beautiful woman (not Carla), and enough money to one day buy a yacht big enough to sail around the world.

My co-workers and I would hear of his dream time and again during coffee breaks or while waiting for freight to come in. There was a darker side to Banana Bob that he didn't talk about. The word was that he had some connection to the mob. But nobody would talk about the mob, if you knew what was good for you. You certainly didn't mention names, unless and until they were dead, and then in the hushed tones reserved for the "men of respect."

Banana Bob never got a chance to fulfill his dream. He was killed in an accident when a truck crushed him against the loading platform. At least, they said it was an accident, but who knows with "made men," those fully initiated in the secret society.

The funeral was lavish enough, but no burial at sea. Carla had him cremated. I remember the silver gleaming urn among the flowers and wondering if Carla would have a private ceremony some time later. That was before the parade of mistresses stopped before the urn with teary faces that turned Carla livid. "That bastard," she said to her son, "Even at his funeral he has to mortify me."

I saw Carla at the Pathmark several months later and told her about how Banana Bob always wanted to be buried at sea. "Well, he's sleeping with the fishes now," she said. "He's slept with every dame in every port he's put in."

"Oh, did you cast his ashes off the Highlands as he always wanted?"

"Not exactly," she said. "I was so angry at the funeral that I brought his ashes home and dumped them into the aquarium in the living room. Finally, I got him to stay at home."

There's a bumper sticker that says, "Be nice to your children. They are the ones who will choose your nursing home." One could also say, "Be nice to your wife. She's the one who will choose your final resting place."

It occurs to me that Jesus had no financial planner, never bought term insurance (but offered universal life policies), and did not make pre-need funeral arrangements. He was buried in a grave that wasn't his own, though one could argue that it was only a short-term loan. Yet Jesus had a firm fix on what was important in life.

In the nineteenth and early part of the twentieth century, the great theological question seems to have been "What must I do to be saved?" Now, at the beginning of a new millennium, the questions seem to be, "What must I do to be relevant?" "What is the purpose of my life?" What really does matter? Was Banana Bob's promiscuity a superficial expression of a deep need for a meaningful relationship that he felt he could not achieve with Carla?

Jean-Paul Sartre said that "hell is other people," but that holds out the possibility of communication and relationship. The Buddhist believes that heaven is oblivion, where there is no awareness, just being. If I were

## BANANA BOB SLEEPS WITH THE FISHES

designing hell, it would be a place of total whiteness, devoid of any color, any substance, any person—only the awareness of self.

Banana Bob sought an eternity of pleasure based on his earthly experiences. Most concepts of heaven involve relationships, especially with God. Hell, as Dante said, is without hope, without mercy, without the knowledge of a loving God who surely would not withhold forgiveness and love.

# CHASING GYPSIES

"What do you want to be when you grow up?"

There are times now when I wish I could have answered that question with, "I don't want to grow up. I enjoy being a child and not having to worry about earning a living, being responsible for others, making a contribution to a society, or fulfilling a destiny." Peter Pan was able to return to Never-Neverland, but I, like most people I knew, had to leave the child's world of fantasy to take up residence in the "real" world.

While we inhabit that dwelling place of wonder and imagination, we begin the process of discernment, of deciding what we want to do with our lives. How many factors enter into our choosing? Do we satisfy our unfulfilled needs for adventure or intellectual curiosity? Do we succumb to our appetites for the accumulation of things, or wealth, or power and influence? Is there an altruistic rumbling that spurs us on to service? Are our choices made for us by parents or friends or by opportunistic circumstances?

There are several words that are used to describe what we do with our lives. Some people have jobs, some have careers, some have professions, some have vocations, and some have combinations of these.

I am not certain where the term "job" originated, but I have always associated it with that great sufferer of the Old Testament, Job, who said "we are born into pain, even as the sparks fly upward." His life was one of misery and travail. A person who works at what he does and calls it simply a job often sees it as something to be done to earn enough money to free him to do what he really would prefer to be doing.

I had jobs while I was in high school that were simply that—jobs. I never really hated them, but I knew fully well that I didn't want to spend the rest of my life delivering newspapers, working on the docks, driving a truck, or working in a freezer loading ice cream trucks. But they provided me with the money that I needed to buy books, put gas in the car, date girls, and save for an education. They also gave me wonderful opportunities to make mistakes, an essential ingredient in that most desirable of qualities for job applications—experience. But more than anything else, I came into contact with other people, wise guys and wise men, who taught me much, mostly unintentionally.

My father wanted me to pursue a career as a corporate lawyer because "that's where the money is." Those who were raised during the depression tended to see wealth as the standard by which you gauged a person's worth. A "career" is aptly named because it comes from the French word meaning "to run around in circles." I wasn't interested in a career.

I was responding to a vocation (from the Latin *vocare*, "to call"). There was something inside of me that was calling me to my life's work, but I wasn't sure what it was saying. I had an interest in the professional theater and had demonstrated some skill in acting. I felt the allure of classical archaeology and had imagined myself uncovering the remnants of vanished civilizations. Later I discovered that these were not vocations, but avocations, which were calling me away from what I really felt I had to do with my life.

We don't always hear a clear call to our destiny. Sometimes, like the prophet Samuel, it is a whisper in the night that grows louder as we respond and say, "Here I am." There are times, however, when it is not so much a call as a push. Like a reluctant Jonah we have to be pursued and have other doors slam in our face before we realize that we are meant to walk a different path.

Men and women often enter the service and healing professions to heal themselves as well as the people they serve. I have known psychologists, priests, ministers, and social workers who were conflicted about unresolved issues from their past, whether the guilt they bore for deeds done or the pain inflicted upon them by others. The "wounded healer" that Henri Nouen describes is not only hurt by those whom he would heal, but identifies with those who suffer and is able to heal because he himself is hurting.

Johann, the German in Israel studying to become a rabbi was not born a Jew, but raised in a good Lutheran family. The Holocaust had made such an impact upon his life and burdened him with so much angst that he felt the only way he could atone for the sins of his culture, which he bore personally, was to become the very thing his country had persecuted. His eyes welled with tears whenever he told his story, and I saw in him the Christ who becomes one of us in order to know our pain.

The circumstances into which we are born often point us in a certain direction, but our lives are also shaped by people we have known and our life experiences. Casual remarks made in passing become seeds that take root. Experiences and events that are thrust upon us and that seem incidental at the time become life-transforming.

There is no such thing as a normal family. Beaver Cleaver's household would be considered dysfunctional by today's standards. Our families shape who we are by how they function, or do not function. My parents were divorced when I was in my early teens and my two brothers and I were each raised in slightly different environments and came under the influence of different family members. Bob, the youngest, spent more time with the Serio branch and eventually decided to become a priest. George operated within my father's sphere of influence and followed the path of labor, pension, and healthcare administration. I found refuge in the care and understanding of church people at my mother's church, St. Stephan's, who were both tolerant and encouraging. They helped me channel my acting skills into preaching. I learned to become sensitive to the pain of the world, but found it more difficult to be sensitive to individuals. When you have experienced so much pain in your own life, you either become more adept at detecting it in others, or you become immune to it. We need to share our stories and listen to the stories of others lest we become insensitive as a field of stones touching each other on the hard exteriors of our existence without knowing the core of who we are.

My first real job after the newspaper circulation business was at the age of fourteen. My father had a job as a dispatcher for the Terminal Cartage Company, operated by the Port of New York Authority. He hired me to load and unload trucks. My first day on the job was an introduction to the netherworld of daily criminal activity that seemed to go on under the noses of persons who looked the other way, or just didn't want to get involved. The FBI arrived during my first coffee break. I thought they were there because I was four years under the legal age for working, but they were investigating the theft of a skid of nickel bars consigned to the United States Mint. No one knew what had happened—neither the driver nor the dock workers nor management. The skid just vanished and the insurance company paid for it.

## CHASING GYPSIES

A dockworker handed me a business card. It was a picture of the three Chinese monkeys: "Hear Nothing; See Nothing; Say Nothing." The word got around fast. "Keep your mouth shut if you know what's good for you!" Above all, don't ask questions.

This applied especially to the constant stream of goods offered in the parking lot. Someone was always showing up with a trunk full of swag that "fell off the truck"—clothing, electronics, jewelry, whatever you wanted.

One of the summer help, a college guy with brains but little commonsense, bought a shortwave radio for a few bucks and then filled in the warranty card and mailed it in. "Are you crazy," yelled the seller. " I hope you didn't put my name on that card in the place where it was bought."

Working on the docks provided a well-rounded education. I learned geography—the towns and states and the truck lines that served them. I learned physics and Archimedes's principle of how to apply leverage and why you should not put heavy boxes on top of a load. My language skills improved with the addition of a very colorful and descriptive vocabulary that I would have to unlearn as I moved into more genteel society. The psychology of human behavior and cultural anthropology were the lessons from which I benefitted most.

The men on the docks were mostly Italian Americans, primarily second-generation Americans who still knew how to speak their native tongue. Mike Santoramos was in his mid-seventies. On hot summer nights he would be gasping for air as he pushed his handtruck. The guys yelled at him constantly that he would have a heart attack and that he should retire. He was still working when I left for seminary and probably outlived many of his co-workers.

I liked his name—Santoramos—Italian for "Holy Branch." I kidded him that it sounded like "Santoranos—"Holy Frog." He didn't like that. He didn't talk much to anyone because of his poor English.

Another Mike had a severe cleft lip and palate that had never been treated. He knew English very well, but couldn't speak it. His cleft lip and lack of teeth made him impossible to understand. He was ridiculed mercilessly. One day a driver turned up with a dog that barked like he had a hare-lip. All night long you would hear the men yelling, "Hey, Mike—moof, moof, moof."

Toby, the forklift driver, had his own regulation uniform—a torn undershirt with spaghetti stains. He was usually slovenly and unshaven. He knew where to hide from the dock bosses and could conceal the forklift in the midst of piles of freight. Sometimes work in several trucks would be stopped completely until Toby could be found and roused from his naps. The loud shouts and acclamations of profanity would echo down the dock.

Tony was a three-pack-a-day smoker of unfiltered Camels who must have had a morbid fear of living forever. He had been moonlighting on the dock while going to police academy, aspiring to be a member of the elite Hudson County Police Department. I don't know why it was so elite, since its jurisdiction was limited to only one street, Hudson Blvd. in Jersey City, and only apprehended traffic violators and perhaps some petty criminals. Nevertheless, Tony had us believing that he would be North Jersey's answer to its increasing crime rate. Just the thought of Tony with a gun was enough to make you cringe.

Tony did make the police force and carried a gun. But one day he was too fast on the draw and shot himself in the foot. I had heard that he had become a guard at Roosevelt Stadium controlling crowds at high school football games.

Wild Bill had a face that had been rearranged many times in many bars. The stereotypical Irish brawler, he had acquired a taste for strong whiskey, but much preferred quantity over quality. I wondered why he bothered having an apartment since he seemed to wake up every morning in a strange location and in the bed of some woman he hadn't known twenty-four hours previously.

Wild Bill was a bodybuilder, short and strong as an ox. If there was something heavy that had to be moved and you couldn't find Toby, you called for Wild Bill. Bill relished demonstrating his strength. His idol was Hercules, and Bill had seen every Steve Reeves movie. He would test me on my knowledge of Greek mythology and Roman military tactics. It wasn't much of a test, since his knowledge was based on the Hollywood version. When Bill married Sandy from the office, we thought he would settle down, but whiskey was his aqua vita and he continued his ways. The last I heard of him he had been picked up for wearing a Nazi helmet and goose-stepping down Wilson Avenue at four in the morning.

A fifty-year retrospective of these men I knew for such a short period has turned them into caricatures, emphasizing not necessarily their most dominant personality trait, but that which was revealed through the windows of those particular summers. I saw only that which was highlighted by the perspective of others who also had flawed vision.

# CHASING GYPSIES

Do we really know one another? We reveal what we want others to see. We see what we choose to see. We hold up the lenses of our own prejudices and ask others to look through them.

When I think of Mike Santoramos, I wish I could go back and sit down with him and learn of his family, what had brought him to America, and why he needed to work so late in life. I wish I could have penetrated the suspicion of Harelip Mike to really know how he felt about the ridicule that was heaped upon him. Did he ever know the love of a woman? Had he ever loved someone, or was his love rejected? How much crying did he do inside? How much anger was pent up in that strong body?

Toby came in one day to pick up his check. He was clean-shaven and wore a new white shirt. I didn't recognize him, but I realized that there was another side to him that most of us never knew.

Was Wild Bill trying to live up to the myth that others projected on him and that he helped cultivate? We create roles for ourselves. As in ancient Greek tragedies we wear the masks and then become the persons we choose to play, encouraged by others who have also been convinced of that role. We then live out the expectations of others.

Working on the docks was hard work, but the pay was good—not as much as a driver, but more than a helper. I liked the helper jobs. You rode around with the driver and assisted him in unloading the freight. Best of all was working with "gypsies," for which you received drivers' pay for doing the work of a helper.

Union rules at the time would not permit a long-haul driver from coming into a territory and depriving one of the local union men of a day's pay. So these drivers had to take along a local union man and pay him what the union demanded for a driver's wages, even though he didn't drive the truck. He wasn't even required to know how to drive. He just went along and assisted if necessary. Sometimes independent drivers, working alone and not operating for a major truck line, would try to make clandestine deliveries themselves. In the trade they were known as gypsies. If a union man could identify these gypsies and prove that they were depriving someone of work, he could claim a day's pay for doing nothing. There were a few men who made a career of not working by "chasing gypsies."

I usually worked the second shift at Consolidated Freightways. This gave me time to get things done in the afternoon and to sleep later in the morning. One late summer day, I received a call from my father who told me to go over to the Durkees Company and pick up a check. Someone had spotted two gypsies, but could only claim one. It was all perfectly legal according to the rules, but it just didn't seem right. I tried to get out of it by saying my car wasn't working.

Dad couldn't believe his idiot son. "Then call a cab, for Christ's sake. For a couple of dollars cab fare you can get a day's pay."

There is something about taking a cab to a job you don't have to pick up a paycheck that you didn't earn that raises issues of morality and work ethic. I wonder what John Calvin would say about this. But I already knew deep in my soul. Earning your bread by the sweat of your brow was honest labor, and so was handling freight. But we move away from the straight and narrow by inches and by fine print until we are no longer certain what good work is and what is not. I was convinced to get out of the business. Sometimes a call is a loud "No!"

# ANGELS DESCENDING

"Years from now when you talk about this—be kind."

—Laura Reynolds in Robert Sherwood's
 *Tea and Sympathy*

WE HAD TO BE careful with nuts. Bob always had problems digesting certain foods. The sight of a walnut cake after dinner would send him into hysterical raving. When Bob showed the first signs of illness, we thought it might be ulcers or an allergic reaction. For a time he presented the fiction that it might be Chrohn's Disease, and then, as serious as it was, cancer. We left it at that.

Even then, Bob had kept his lifestyle to himself and said that he had contracted an incurable disease from blood transfusions while being treated for ulcers. We all had our own versions of the secret, but the unspoken and unnamed "thing" dwelt in the shadows. Bob was dying. How was not important. "Why?" wasn't asked. We simply wanted to savor what little time remained.

On a hot summer day, Bob drove to Pennsylvania to tell me the news. We kept in touch by phone, and visits to Newark became more frequent, but they were never often enough or long enough. They never are.

When Bob entered the hospital for the last time, not knowing it was for the last time but fearing it might be, he was a tyrant, a king issuing commands who could not command death. It was fear, with occasional flashes of faith—or the reverse. He must have been anointed by his priest friends a hundred times over, but all the masses and all the "Aves" could not keep death from his door.

Bob bestowed his possessions, making a list of who was to receive what. George received his coin collection. "You get the stamp collection," he said. I thought of all the lonely hours he had spent assembling them and how he acquired them. They are now things that sit in the bags I brought them home in. "Sell them," Bob had told me, "they're valuable." I haven't. Time is much more precious than wealth, and we never have enough time.

When it was time to clean out Bob's apartment I found it to be a shrine to St. Anthony, the patron saint of things lost. I remembered the prayer Catholic children prayed when they were searching for something misplaced: "St. Anthony, St. Anthony, please come around; something is lost that cannot be found." Here they were—all the things that were "lost" in our family: Aunt Elsie's books, Mom's pictures, the contents of Dad's wallet, family mementoes that told us who we were.

We lost them and didn't realize what we had lost. Like aspects of ourselves, we become diminished by degrees and by neglect.

I was happy to find this trove of family antiquity and grateful that they had found a place to be gathered. In looking through the contents of Bob's papers, books, and letters from friends, I not only discovered who he was, but who I was, and what we had lost but now in these last days had found—the common threads of our brotherhood.

On my last visit, Bob asked for prayer and "the laying on of hands." I put my hand over his forehead to feel for his aura, the electromagnetic force field that surrounds each person that reiki masters and *qigong* practitioners can manipulate and induce healing and that many cultures have sworn produced therapeutic effects. Bob would have none of this. He seized my hand and held it to his forehead. He wasn't interested in healing energy. He wanted direct human contact. I felt like the archbishop who was about to crown Napoleon, only to have the emperor seize the crown and place it upon his own head. Bob was desperate and was grasping for healing any way he could get it.

In the months before his death, Bob lived in the presence of angels. The previous Christmas he spoke about angelic visitations. He said that a few years ago, while sitting alone in his apartment, he felt a strong urge to visit a friend who was dying of AIDS. It was during a severe March blizzard when he was thankful to be indoors and had no real urgency to go forth into swirling snow and howling winds.

Yet the gnawing need was so great that Bob telephoned another friend, Mike, a local priest, and the two of them drove from North Jersey to

# ANGELS DESCENDING

Manhattan. The streets were almost impassible, and somewhere near Canal Street they got stuck in the drifting snow. It was 3:30 in the morning and there was no one to help.

And then, as if conjured by a desperate prayer, a man suddenly appeared out of a doorway—one of New York's innumerable homeless seeking shelter where he could find it. Without gloves to protect him from the icy cold, the bearded man began to push the car. As they gained traction and moved away, Bob and Mike looked back to wave and thank their benefactor, but there was nobody there. Bob turned to Mike and said, "Angel."

The two men, the priest and the one who had studied for the priesthood, arrived at the apartment in time to give Tommy the last rites of the church and to help him pass from this life to the next. Perhaps Bob and Mike were directed and protected by angels, but I also believe they too became angels to Tom. Angels are those persons, spiritual beings, whether in this world or in the world beyond this one, who do the bidding of God, who render help in times of need, and who give us insight into eternal truth.

At forty-two, Bob was not ready for death; there was too much of life to be lived. Yet, when he realized how tenuous and uncertain life can be, and that his time was being measured out in teaspoons, he called upon his angels for that indomitable courage that helped him face the pain of his illness and his impending mortality. While there were certainly times of fear and anxiety, the test of faith is not only to endure those times, but to prevail—and he did.

I have learned from my brother that we never live for ourselves, but for what we mean to others. The purpose of our own lives is so often the part it plays in the lives of those whom we care for and who care for us. Bob taught me not only to value my time, but especially my relationships. Every friend was precious to him. He often quoted from Antoine de Saint-Exupéry, where the fox says to the "Little Prince" that it is the time you spend on your rose that makes it valuable to you. Bob spent time on his friends and family—a card, a phone call, a visit, just being there. We all knew we were important to him—and we loved him for it.

Bob had a great love of music and singing. He had an excellent voice and a special gift for imitation. He did a fantastic "Ethel Merman." He possessed an incredible storehouse of facts. He remembered the minutiae of family history, details from obscure films, the theater, the history of Newark, or whatever. He knew everything, and he was always right. Even if his facts were wrong, he was always right.

# THE DWELLING PLACE OF WONDER

I loved him for his wackiness—that was one of the gifts he inherited from my father, and a recessive trait of the Serios. There will never be a Christmas without our remembering Bob in his tree costume. Some Christmas past, he designed a suit of green felt and wired it with Christmas lights. Perched on top of a green hood was a large star that twinkled on and off. Bob would put on his Christmas tree suit and seek out roadside locations where he had access to electricity and stand by the side of the road waving at motorists. The reactions were usually of delight, but I always had the fear that someone would toss cold water on his Christmas cheer and short-circuit his love of celebration. He was an electric eccentric who could bring laughter to almost every occasion, including funerals.

A raconteur of the first order, to engage Bob in repartee was to enter a battle of wits with less than a full arsenal. He was a master of the quick rejoinder and delighted in the fast pun. A conversation with him was sure to be lively. But his spirituality ran deep. Our discussions on theology and ecclesiology, while sending Emilio to his easel to escape the dialogue, were stimulating and enlightening. We shared our insights into the nature of spiritual reality; he appreciated my investigations into mystical states of consciousness, and I appreciated his fascination with angels.

In the final weeks of his life, I thought about Jacob's dream at Bethel and the ladder of angels ascending and descending. The gate of heaven was opened. The descending angels had been present with him throughout his final weeks: the unseen cloud that surrounded him from the heavenly world, as well as the very real angels that ministered to him through the days and nights of his affliction.

The descending angels remind us that it is upon the ashes of our yesterdays that we must forge new tomorrows. We never forget those who have left our world—their influence and presence are still with us—but the rest of our lives must be lived in the future. That is where our God leads us.

# BUTTERFLY WINGS

Dr. Henry Donn was chairman of the high school athletic department. I was hanging out in his office one day waiting for the football coach and Dr. Donn was looking through his desk for a couple of postage stamps.

"Why don't you run down to the post office and get me a sheet of stamps. Mail these two letters and bring me the rest."

When I returned with the sheet of stamps minus two for the mailing, Dr. Donn was greatly annoyed. "Out of the four corners," he said, "you had to use the stamps with the numbers."

"I'm sorry," I replied, "I didn't know you were a philatelist."

"What did you call me?" He glared in shocked disbelief.

"I said I didn't know you collected stamps."

"Get the hell out of here."

I noticed the smirk on health teacher Paul Bogatko's face. I learned later that I had called Dr. Donn, not a philatelist, but a "fellatialist." I was learning about sex through trial and error.

I was one of Bert's Boys. Bert Manhoff was the football coach, and in those days East Side was a football powerhouse. Those on the team were heroes, admired by little boys and big girls alike. And Bert held his players to the highest standards, both academically, morally, and socially. While I had given up football in my freshman year, I remained with the team as statistician and analyst.

Bert cornered me in the corridor just after midterm reports were distributed and asked to see my card. I showed it to him—all A's and one C in trigonometry. He pushed me up against the wall and started berating me for my failure to meet his standards. "You can do much better than that," he bellowed. Now, I knew that Bert was relieved that his star quarterback would not have to leave the team because he had just managed to pass his midterm exams. Why was he getting on my back when I was nothing to the team?

"I expect better from you because you are capable of better," he said. Those were good words and when I failed to listen to them I always felt guilty. I have often thought of how much of what I have done in life was the result of living up to someone else's expectations, or of what I imagine God expects of me.

When Bert died, I sent an email to his son, a rabbi in San Leandro, California. I told him of his father's kindness and faith in his students and, though he was demanding and difficult to play for, he would do anything for his boys. When I graduated, I received a scholarship from B'Nai Brith. I later joked with the coach that a Jewish organization was helping a Christian pursue a theological education. He never admitted it, but I have always felt that he had something to do with that scholarship. His faith was a seed that grew in many young men. We toss our pebbles in the pond and never know what distant shores the ripples reach.

My colleague, Bob Rhoads, used to say that some of the good old boys in the Reading Ministerium who knew him and his father used to pull him aside and say, "Now Bobby, we expect great things of you." That's not a bad thing to say to anyone. We are all accountable to each other and responsible to our past, not out of a sense of guilt, but out of a sense of keeping faith. If it is expected of us in our religion that we are to "do justice, love mercy, and walk humbly with our God," then we try to be true to that tradition and fulfill that destiny.

Those who taught me most likely have forgotten some of the challenges that they have laid before my path. Bert Manhoff may very well have forgotten that incident a month later, but to this day I am still trying to live up to his expectations of being better than I am and doing better than I have done.

Sensitivity to others is not a trait one readily acquires in the city. To the contrary, the city teaches you to look out for yourself, to watch your back, to trust no one, and to be insensitive to the feelings of others. Bernie Halperin taught drama, but he also taught awareness. He introduced me to the theater and the mechanics of portraying emotions and insight into personality.

Bernie would arrange class trips to the great Rodgers and Hammerstein musicals at the Papermill Playhouse in Millburn and many excursions

# BUTTERFLY WINGS

to the theater in New York. It was on one such occasion that I learned a little about sensitivity.

We had arrived early for a performance of "Our Town" at the Circle in the Square in the Village. We had some time to spare so we wandered around the neighboring streets. I was looking through some books at a book stall on Christopher Street when I heard a familiar voice. I looked up and directly across from me was Rod Steiger discussing the merits of a particular book with his then wife, Claire Bloom. I forget the book in question, but I knew something about it and offered my bit of insight to the esteemed actor. He stared at me with the kind of look that said high school students should not offer opinions to famous actors unless asked, and then moved on. I continue to admire his work, but that brief stare told me much more about the man and about myself and how we interpret the body language of others.

I was with Bernie a few minutes later when we happened to run into Tom DiAndrea, a chemistry teacher at East Side. Bernie told Tom what he was doing in New York with his drama class and that they were waiting for the performance. Assuming that DiAndrea had other things to do, Bernie kiddingly invited him to see the play with us. Tom took him up on it and followed us to the theater.

There were no tickets available. I remember the hurt, disappointment, and embarrassment on the face of Tom DiAndrea. Bernie, of course, expressed his regret. We learn sensitivity in many ways. I don't know if this had any lasting effect on Bernie Halperin, but for me it was one of the slices of living that we ignore at the time, though it shapes our future and makes us what we are. If the flapping of a butterfly's wings in South America creates a storm in Europe and sets in motion forces that continue through time affecting centuries to come, how much more sensitive should we be to the people and events around us who make us what we are?

Nick DiNardo was still playing his string bass in restaurants and for wedding receptions following his retirement from the music department and the high school orchestra. I took a class called "Instrumental Practice" with him.

I am not a musician. I have long since forgotten how to read music, if ever I did. The earliest attempt anyone made at trying to get me to play an instrument was in third grade when Mr. Nervola handed me a "flute-a-phone." It made an awful noise and I soon gave it up. It seems the only thing I learned about music in elementary school was that violin bows used horse hair.

I took DiNardo's class without having an instrument in mind. He suggested I consider the string bass. "You don't think that I'm going to carry that back and forth to school, do you?" When he said "No," I then gave it some serious thought. It would certainly prevent me from spending a lot of after-school hours practicing. But then again, I couldn't very well play the string bass in the marching band. So I settled for the trumpet.

I hadn't had the instrument a month when Nick asked me to march in the Columbus Day Parade. "Are you out of your mind," I said, forgetting that he was my teacher. "Sure, I'd like to be in the parade, but I can't play this thing yet."

DiNardo just smiled. "I don't want you to play, just walk and fake it. We need people to fill out the formation." It turned out to be the second-best performance in my short-lived musical career. The best came the following semester after I had dropped instrumental practice and taken voice training with Emily Wilder.

Emily Wilder looked like a spear-carrier in a Wagnerian opera and had the voice of a Valkyrie to match. She put us through rigorous vocal dynamics that seemed silly to guys who hung out with the football team. All of the students in her class were accomplished singers and members of the chorus, including one who had gone on to state competition. The only thing I had known about music was that you are supposed to sing louder when the black dots went up the lines and softer when they went down. At least Nick DiNardo had corrected that misunderstanding.

By the end of the semester Mrs. Wilder had recommended me for an award as the most improved singer in the entire class. That was a snap, considering where I had started from. My grand debut came at the awards ceremony for commencement. The entire upper classes were gathered in the auditorium and more than two hundred of my classmates were in the front row. We were doing a selection of Civil War songs and I was in the front row of a sixty-voice choir.

After a medley of songs by the choir, it was my turn in the spotlight. A microphone was brought out to center stage. The orchestra began their intro and the choir started to hum the "Battle Hymn of the Republic." I stepped down from the choir and moved to the microphone. The gasps from my classmates were audible, and then the whispers, and finally the stunned silence as they waited for me to sing.

## BUTTERFLY WINGS

Only I didn't. But I gave one of the best readings of the Gettysburg Address ever heard on that stage. Bernie Halperin suggested that I should really consider the theater. I went into the ministry instead, and at times I have failed to notice the difference.

# WORDSWORTH WILLIAMS

WORDSWORTH WILLIAMS HAD BEEN teaching English at East Side High School for more years than he should have. He was well past retirement age and out of place in the mid-1950's. Like many others of the aging teaching establishment at the school, his time had passed. The torch, the symbol of learning that was East Side's icon, had been reduced to a few burning embers. Yes, there were many who still wanted to get as good an education as possible in this city that was just beginning to see the dark clouds of racial unrest gather. The white population of Newark in the postwar years had begun its migration to the suburbs, leaving a tired and worn infrastructure to poor blacks who were at the mercy of the white politicos in city hall. The mood was changing in the city and it could be felt in the classroom.

I remember Mr. Williams as I would have remembered Mr. Chips had he existed and been my teacher. With a name like Wordsworth Williams he could be nothing other than a teacher of English. I was in his freshman English class where the subject was mythology. It was to become a life-long interest.

In a sense I grew up with mythology, the fables and stories of the ancient Greeks and Romans blended with tales from the Bible. The enduring value of myth is its layers and textures. You can revisit myth at various times in your life and continue to learn its ancient truth even as you discover new ones. Eventually, when you achieve enlightenment, you realize that the truth is not in the myth but in you; the myth is simply a mirror that helps you see it.

The layers of truth that my parents would see in these stories were not the verities that I would discover. My father would often quiz me on my knowledge of mythology. One night, after dinner, he asked me, "Who is no one?" What a deep philosophical question coming from this ex-prizefighter! "Is this a riddle?" I asked. "No," he said, "Who is no man?" Well, that was a little different, but I still didn't know the answer. The question was an absurdity, a contradiction, a conundrum: the "who" implies the existence of one who does not exist. He laughed as I tried various convoluted reasonings to what he considered a very straightforward answer.

"No Man" is the false name Odysseus gave when the cyclops Polyphemus asked him who he was, so that later when Polyphemus was blinded by Odysseus and his fellow cyclopes asked who was hurting him, he could only reply, "No Man is hurting me."

How many times have I revisited that story and saw within it paradigms of cunning, human identity, semantics, strategy, and more. Wordsworth Williams introduced me to many more stories with the same effect. I would have loved to have sat at his feet and listened to him reach back into his own history, his own personal mythology, and bring forth the lessons of his life to be passed on to a newer generation.

Unfortunately, the barbarians were at the gates. The students in his class were disrespectful of this gentle soul who never learned the art of disciplining students because he expected students to want to learn. When he called their chronic tardiness to their attention, they would ridicule him and hurl their invectives and expletives with greater force. When he tried to talk of Aphrodite and Ares, they spoke of sex and gang fights. When he attempted to relate ancient myth to contemporary culture, they mocked him for his irrelevancy. There was nothing he could do to stem the rising tide of youthful banality.

The gates were finally breached, and, like Archimedes standing naked before the Roman sword of ignorance, Mr. Williams finally came to the end of his career. He was retelling the beautiful story of Baucis and Philemon, the elderly couple who were the only ones to recognize the divine visitation of Zeus and Hermes. The chatter in the back of the room grew increasingly louder. "Boring." "What crap." Mr. Williams asked for silence so he could make his point. The point of a paper airplane hit him in the face. The point was made. There were tears in his eyes as he calmly got up from his desk and left the room. We had substitute teachers for the remainder of the semester.

How do we recognize beauty when we confront it? How do we know truth even when it is put before us? "Unless someone guides me, how can I know," said the Ethiopian eunuch to the Apostle Philip. Unless we have good teachers and mentors and guides, how can we know the way? The entirety of human evolution may be carried in our genes, but the wisdom of all of earth's past civilizations must be relearned in every new age. We are only a flashpoint away from what we once were.

The sack of Rome by the barbarian hordes, the burning and pillaging of Constantinople by the civilized Christian crusaders, the burning of the library at Alexandria by a caliph who said that all wisdom can be found in the Koran and that if it's not there, it isn't wisdom—those were major setbacks for the advancement of human wisdom and learning. We have subtler ways to heap ridicule and scorn on those with wisdom and vision in our own day. "There are none so blind as those who will not see." We need to value the repositories of wisdom as well as wisdom itself.

# GHOSTS

I BELIEVE IN GHOSTS. Ghosts come in different forms. There are ghosts that haunt houses and frighten little children. There are ghosts of the mind, the residue of the past that must be dealt with in a different way before one can move on in life.

For thirty years we had been coming down to North Carolina and staying at my brother-in-law's house. Whether it was a week or two, we would share in his life, through the trials and tribulations of raising a son, through three separate marriages and the hard lessons of life gained from those encounters, through the moves from a ranch-style house in a family neighborhood to a year-round vacation house on the inlet to his bachelor retirement home in a closed estate. In his later years, Bill would come to Pennsylvania and give us the keys to his house. He would stay with his aged mother while Mary Ann and I would come to his home near the beach where I could catch up on my reading, do some writing, and plan for the coming year.

When Bill died of cancer in the early part of 1997, we were very hesitant about coming to his home. Mom would be cared for, we were assured by our daughter, but we felt strange about coming to Bill's house knowing that he was no longer a part of it. His son, Alan, had gone through it shortly after his death and removed much of the accumulated detritus of his life. Most of the important things were still there—not just the furniture, but the mementos of his life: his diploma from Penn State in Industrial Engineering, a farewell portrait and valedictory from his friends at a plant in Florida, wall hangings that Mary Ann had made for him.

From the moment I took a cup from the cupboard or a beer from the fridge, my thoughts were that Bill wouldn't be coming back to this house when we returned to Pennsylvania, and yet there were the signs, and even feelings of his presence. How much of ourselves do we infuse into the material things that are a part of our lives. When I saw Teddy Roosevelt's *pince-nez* glasses on a table in his house on Sagamore Hill I felt that his persona was still in and around that personal object. In the same way I feel Bill's essence in the things that he used and touched. Perhaps this is why it is so hard to get rid of the accumulation of a lifetime, whether our own or those close to us. We become a part of the things that are a part of us.

We were very grateful for the box of photographs that Alan sent to us. Here were hundreds of snapshots tossed into an old shoebox, the events of a lifetime accumulating over the years: Stuart's first haircut, Tasha opening a Christmas present, Matthew's first encounter with a wave at the shore. Here they were, fragments of memories preserved in a moment frozen in time.

Also in the box were other photos, much older—snapshots of experiences that no one living can remember. They must have been important at the time, but now are almost useless because we can't attribute any meaning to them. Perhaps another generation will look at these pictures the way we look at the faces that peer at us from the nineteenth century and will wonder who they were, what were their names, what were their lives like, what were their hopes and dreams.

What will happen to the events of our own lives? Will they, too, be gone forever when we who remember them are gone? Will we, too, a hundred years from now be nothing more than a faded photograph, a dim memory in a descendant's faltering recollection? It's hard to imagine that each one of us will one day be an ancestor.

The photographs have taught me that things and events only have meaning in the context of other people with whom we have had a relationship. The people we love continue to live as we are reminded of them in the images and ghosts of our conjuring. Life is relationships with people. There are times when those relationships must be suspended for a time, or at least changed in the way they are expressed.

Ghosts come and go, but they have no permanent residence in our world. And neither should we hold on to them for long. Eternity is time enough for that.

# A TRICKLE OF BLOOD IN THE GUTTER

I WALKED THE EIGHT city blocks to school each day crossing the streets of the presidents. We lived on Monroe Street, next to the vitamin factory. Newark's water and air wasn't all that great. Someone once bottled a perfume called "Eau de Newark." It didn't sell—even as a souvenir. But if you had to breathe city air, it seemed healthier to breathe in vitamin smells rather than some other unknown toxins.

My daily progression to school wasn't seven miles up hill both ways, but it was a good mile walk. After Monroe came Adams, Jackson, Van Buren, Polk, and finally Wilson Avenue on which our school was located.

The main route that intersected the presidents was Ferry Street. In an earlier century it would have proceeded down "Dutch Neck" to the ferry at Newark Bay that would cross to Manhattan. People in the Ironbound section would be known as "down-neckers." For those of us who lived on one of the presidential streets off Ferry, it might take an hour or more to walk home because there was so much to see and do on Ferry Street. One could stop at the Rivoli and see the movie stills and posters of coming attractions, or the toys in Lorzak's window, or break for a vanilla Coke at the luncheonette.

Between Jackson and Adams you could have your shoes fixed while you waited in two-foot high cubicles with swinging doors to give you privacy in case you had holes in your socks. If you wanted to see the skeletal outline of your feet, you could put your foot in a fluoroscope machine which would tell mothers how tight a fit their children's shoes were.

In this same block was the barber shop, one of my father's hangouts. Pat Diacova had four barber chairs, but seldom did he have more than two barbers working. This was convenient for Dad. He would come in through the back door, help himself to Pat's lunch, and then sack out in the last chair until Pat was ready for him.

I didn't like going to Pat's for a haircut because I didn't care much for his selection of magazines. But since Dad was paying for it, I didn't have much choice.

Pat noticed that my hair was starting to thin and came up with the brilliant idea of setting my hair on fire. The thinking behind this near immolation was that by singeing the hair, the end would fuse and prevent it from splitting. I enjoyed the celebrity status while the little kids watched in amazement as Pat ran the fire through my hair, perhaps hoping for some greater conflagration. Unfortunately the monthly torching didn't work.

Dad taught me a lot of things he never intended. Quality time with Dad on weekends meant accompanying him in pursuit of floating crap games. Wherever there was a lightly traveled street with a brick wall, you could find a bunch of guys throwing dice. The favorite spots were the back of the Public Bath House on Wilson Avenue or the telephone company building on Van Buren at Chestnut or any location where you could run in more than one direction.

I was given the job of watchdog: "Wait in the car and keep your eyes opened, and yell if you see any cops." It was a cat and mouse game. The cops knew when and where the games were held. They would watch at a distance until there was enough money on the ground, and then they would attack with sirens blaring. There were very few arrests. The intention was to disperse the crap shooters as quickly as possible so that the cops could move in and gather up the abandoned money. If one of the gamblers happened to be caught, he could easily avoid arrest by dropping his wad of bills. It was one of the many perks that went with being a police officer in the city. No one ever complained. I certainly didn't the one time I got left behind and a cop gave me a five dollar bill to keep my mouth shut.

A child's world should be free of violence and war, racial hatred and domestic strife, and all the other ills of humankind. But we don't choose the world into which we are born. We adapt to it as best we can.

Children are not supposed to kill other children as often happens today. Murder was an adult pastime in which children were merely spectators. There were clearly defined borders separating reality from the unreal

# A TRICKLE OF BLOOD IN THE GUTTER

world of violence and mayhem. Killing took place in the movies or on television. (My uncle would say that whenever the television wouldn't work, we had to call the repairman to empty out the dead bodies that accumulated from all the westerns and police shows. The average child today by the age of eighteen will have seen 16,000 murders and 200,000 acts of violence.) Even death in the news was part of another world. Or should have been.

There were far too many deaths that were part of my life—violent deaths that happened to people I knew or who my parents knew. I am often amazed at how casually we dealt with it, as if it were just another topic for discussion at the breakfast table before we got on with the day's activities.

Red was a nice guy, one of the guys who used to hang out at Pepper's store. He had two boys of his own, a regular family man. He offered to take me down to his bungalow at the shore, and I was more than happy to go with his family to Asbury Park. It was a wonderful weekend on the beach, riding in his boat, going on the boardwalk rides. Any time you can get out of the city, see more than asphalt and concrete, and smell salt air rather than Newark air was indeed welcome. Most of my friends came from broken homes, so it was also good to be part of a normal, functional family for a change.

Summer's lease that year seemed shorter. I was back in school when I saw Red's picture in the newspaper. He had been killed in a shootout with the police. There was his bloodied body slumped over the hood of his car. I learned that life was never what it seems to be. Within every family there is hidden pain and sorrow, and a dark side that seldom reveals itself to even close friends and associates. I never knew that Red was a wanted criminal.

It felt good to be back in school, to be in a safe environment where nothing could go wrong. My church, the library, the museum were also safe zones where I would find refuge, but anything can happen on the street.

It was a Friday morning when I took my last walk to school by way of the Ferry Street route. As I crossed Adams Street I saw the police barricades in front of the Beck Hazzard Shoe Store. The pavement was covered with blood, trickling down the curb and into the gutter. I had never seen that much blood before except in the movies.

But this wasn't some *noir* flick. This was real. A small crowd of people had gathered and the police were getting ready to leave. I learned that sometime in the early hours a man had stalked a young beautician and killed her on the spot before putting the gun to his own head.

# THE DWELLING PLACE OF WONDER

Violence and murder in the city are nothing new. It happens every day. It is when you have to step over the blood that it becomes personal and real. Although I didn't know the girl who was murdered, I knew of her and may have seen her. She was a pretty woman. Her killer was a rejected lover who in the passion of a difficult breakup could not see any alternative to the cessation of two lives.

We are both rational and passionate beings. There are times when we act analytically on the basis of our personal philosophy, and there are times when we act impulsively without malice aforethought. Murder and suicide do not seem like rational acts, and I doubt if I could ever be persuaded of their efficacy except in the most extreme of circumstances.

The only emotion I experienced at the time was fear and morbid curiosity. In today's world where urban children suffer depression and anxiety from their exposure to multiple beatings and murders, where children in Uganda or Gaza or Iraq witness terrorist activity almost daily and are often forced to participate in the atrocities of war, one can only imagine how their lives are forever traumatized. They become conditioned to perpetuate the ceaseless cycles of hate and mindless violence.

Certainly not all police officers are corrupt, but when you have experienced more than one on the take, you begin to question authority. Somehow knowing that the United States, statistically one of the more violent nations on earth, is the last remaining super-power, doesn't make me feel any safer. To the contrary, the world is a much more dangerous place than before.

People of faith need to work together for justice and peace, not only to prevent self-annihilation—as if that wouldn't be enough—but because we need to re-establish our true identity as being created in the image of a loving God.

# WALKING THE GOAT

THERE WERE TIMES WHEN I never knew whether my father was creative or just plain nuts, or a little of both. On the way home from school one day, I walked into the restaurant he owned, named "The Office," since that was where he, and many in the neighborhood, conducted much of their business. Dad and his friends were seated at a table set for six. There were five men and one goat.

They were feeding the goat a mixed variety of scraps and commenting on the fact that goats will just about eat anything. Dad reached into his pocket and pulled out a fifty dollar bill and proceeded to feed it to the goat.

Of course I walked in on this scene in the middle of the conversation and didn't know what was going on. Why was this goat at a table in a restaurant? To whom did he belong? Was my father out of his mind putting money in his mouth?

Before I could get answers to these questions, my first reaction was to immediately thrust my hand into the goat's mouth and retrieve the fifty dollar bill. I held the animal firmly and he gagged and finally yielded the piece of paper, but made such a commotion that the waitresses and diners stopped what they were doing to see this incongruous activity. It did not occur to anyone that it was illegal for animals to be in a restaurant, let alone to be served at a table. But they knew my father, and anything was possible with him.

When I unfolded the fifty dollar bill, the laughter increased. It was play money and I was the goat. As for why the animal was in the restaurant, Dad explained that he was a new employee engaged to maintain the little bit of lawn out back—another one of his hare-brained ideas, like the attempt to rent a helicopter to watch a World Series game at Yankee Stadium

# THE DWELLING PLACE OF WONDER

or the impromptu contest at 3 a.m., driving golf balls down Ferry Street with the tees placed in front of St. Stephan's Church.

Now he asked me to take the goat for a walk and handed me a leash. I walked down Wilson Avenue tethered to a goat as passersby stared and drivers honked their horns. Other men and women were walking their dogs, stopping at trees and hydrants, occasionally pausing to engage in conversation with their neighbors. The talk stopped abruptly when this eleven-year-old kid came down the street with a kid looking for patches of grass. I didn't know whether to feel humiliated or to relish the attention that I was getting with my animal act.

Walking the goat taught me that if you want to attract the world's attention, "you've gotta have gimmick," as one famous vaudevillian once said. But once you get their attention, you had better be able to deliver. Dog and pony shows are entertaining, but there is no message. The act is the message, and sometimes it is enough. Walking the goat was a "monstrous" act (from the Latin *monstro*—"to behold in amazement"), the sort of deed that would cause a child to ask, "Mommy, why is that boy walking a goat?" Mommy, of course, would now have the opportunity for a wonderful learning experience with her child.

I sometimes think that wise men, religious leaders, and great teachers often do "crazy" things to communicate eternal truths. Socrates, Jeremiah, Jesus of Nazareth, Lao-tse were all accused of unusual and sometimes antisocial behavior.

But there are also crazy people who do crazy things. It is said that when the student is ready, the teacher appears. And sometimes teachers use bizarre lessons. What we learn in life is dependent not only upon our teachers and the lessons, but the manner in which the lesson is communicated and received. It was certainly unusual to walk the goat. But my father was a wise teacher.

# MURDER IN THE MORNING

IT WAS A BEAUTIFUL, glorious Monday morning—a day bright with sunshine, clarity, and color that enhanced the brilliance of the fall foliage. It was the kind of Monday morning that made you forget that this was the start of another week of meetings, hospital calls, counseling sessions, office work, and all those other details that fill a minister's schedule.

I was just starting to wonder what the *crisis du jour* would be for today as I returned home from an early meeting to review the architect's drawings for a new addition to an apartment complex for seniors of which I was vice president.

I noticed that there was a message on the answering machine. I would deal with this after lunch. As I headed for the door something made me reach over and hit the switch. I stopped in mid-stride when I heard my sister-in-law's voice.

"This is Carole. Something's happened to your father. Call me as soon as possible." I heard the tears in her voice and called her immediately.

"Your father's been shot. In the back of the head. They were waiting for him."

I went numb, the blood draining from my face. My first thoughts were: What is the appropriate response at this time? How should I react? How should I feel? I couldn't say anything and didn't want to know any of the details.

This was an event that I had feared, but prayed would never happen. It was tragedy in the classic sense of a drama that had to play itself out. You knew that it was inevitable, but somehow you hoped that the script could have been rewritten.

# THE DWELLING PLACE OF WONDER

The funeral was magnificent. The flowers lined the walls of the Galante Funeral Home; the stream of mourners was steady. There were the usual expressions, "Sorry for your troubles," "He was such a good man," "How could this happen?," "He was always good to me." I looked into their faces. There were some that were genuinely grief stricken. Some looked angry. And there were one or two who looked like they came just to make sure.

The dignitaries were there: Newark's Mayor Sharpe James and Councilman at large Henry Martinez, Essex County sheriff and later executive Tom D'Allessio, boxing officials and teamster big-wigs—but not those from Local 478 whom the rank and file believed were somehow responsible for the killing of their popular secretary-treasurer and wanted to eliminate from contending in the upcoming election.

There was some speculation as to who did this or why it happened. Someone whispered the advice: "Don't ask. You really don't want to know. It was probably just business." I knew what he meant; I never did ask again. But I would never forget.

My father's death was shocking enough—but two bullets in the back of the head! The medical term would be "a traumatic insult to the brain," but I became aware of the sudden and overwhelming appearance of evil in my life. I had been aware of the nature of tragedy before; "life is suffering" was the first noble truth of Buddhism. I could accept that. But evil was deliberate and intentional, the pulling of a trigger with malice aforethought.

"It was only business," the man said, as though killing someone was an acceptable remedy or solution to someone's dilemma.

Angie asked, "You always knew this was going to happen, didn't you? You knew it would end this way?"

I suppose that deep within me there was always that latent fear. It was something more than a child's fear of abandonment, more than a night terror always lurking under the bed ready to strike at some unexpected moment. If I had read the signs through all the years, perhaps I would have foreseen it. But I didn't want to.

That's the nature of tragedy. There's a certain inevitability to it. It moves toward its conclusion and all the attempts to avoid it or alter its course are to no avail. Jean Anouilh in his play, *Antigone*, has the chorus point out the difference between melodrama and tragedy. With tragedy you have a sense of unavoidable doom, that no matter what a person does, his nature, his environment, his psychological needs that would eventually lead to a foreseeable conclusion—if we are perceptible enough and have the desire to see it. But in most cases we don't.

Although I grew up in a church that came out of the Reformed tradition, I never fully subscribed to the doctrine of predestination. When I was confirmed, Pastor Schlinkmann had assigned me a verse that I was to memorize and recite and that he said I would remember for the rest of my life. He was right about that—I would remember it, but I would not necessarily believe it. The verse was from Ephesians 2:10: "For we are his workmanship, created in Christ Jesus unto good works, which God hath before ordained that we should walk in them."

Of whom was the Apostle Paul speaking when he wrote that—if indeed he had written it? Was he saying that everyone is ordained to do good works? Or that God chooses who will do good and who will do evil and who will do neither?

Was life a role-play, a psycho-drama to be acted out according to a script with scenarios intended to give you insight into what it meant to be human, but coming to an inevitable conclusion? In spite of all the good that he did, all the people he helped, all the lives he touched in positive ways, was my father destined to come to such a traumatic conclusion?

I had known many colleagues who had the mark of inevitable tragedy about them. These were brilliant men who excelled at their craft and were well-liked by friends and parishioners. But there were demons that dwelled within them that drove them to self-destruction.

Steve was a wonderful preacher, but family tragedies propelled him to seek comfort in the arms of a woman not his wife, and so overcome by a sense of guilt and shame, he took his own life by drenching himself in flammable liquid and striking a match.

Mike was at the pinnacle of his career, the pastor of a large church and groomed for denominational leadership, when his affair with his secretary ended his marriage and forced him to resign. He became a successful and wealthy insurance broker until he was sent to prison for embezzling funds and died a broken man.

Roger was also caught in an affair and was on his way to answer charges by his church credentialing committee when he was killed, perhaps intentionally, in an automobile accident with a tractor-trailer.

Paul was knifed to death in his parsonage, the alleged victim of a homosexual relationship gone sour.

Could it have been possible to look into their souls and know what their ultimate destiny would be? Did these men, like so many other men and women, go into their profession to work out their own karma? Did God choose for them or did they choose for themselves their earthly courses that would teach them the lessons that needed to be learned and that would occupy the remainder of their lives?

One would hope that a loving, omniscient God would have some ultimate purpose for human existence and that both good and evil would find its eschatological reconciliation when all things come together at the end. In the end there is only grace, and grace will lead us home.

\* \* \*

The funeral mass at Our Lady of Mount Carmel in Newark was well attended. I participated in the rite, even to the point of concelebrating the Eucharist. I never realized how a small gesture such as raising my hands at the appropriate time to consecrate the sacrament would drive one of the priests up the wall. For a Protestant to join with Roman Catholics in consecrating the Blessed Sacrament was heresy. Most of the concelebrants took it in stride and did not seem to be bothered by my participation. One young priest, however, was apoplectic. "Did you see what he did?" he said to Father Felix, "He can't do that." The other priests managed to calm him down and nothing was said to me at the time. I only learned of this later from Bob who assured me that the archbishop and the pope would never know about this surreptitious attempt to reverse four centuries of schism between Catholics and Protestants.

I gave the funeral eulogy for my father, intending that the good would live after him and that the evil would be interred with his bones. I recalled all of his many virtues: his generosity in helping others, the assistance he gave in helping men find jobs, his pedagogical approach to teaching his children how to cope with life. I reminded the congregation of his warped sense of humor, the fact that he was the only person in the city who could get away with being double-parked on a one-way street facing in the wrong direction, which brought smiles of recognition to his police escort. I mentioned his extensive knowledge of mythology and how his parents wanted him to become a virtuoso violinist. He was on his way to becoming a Renaissance man when he decided not to take violin lessons and deliberately thrust his hand into a cement mixer so that he would have a good excuse to give Luigi.

## MURDER IN THE MORNING

One of *The Star-Ledger*'s particularly obnoxious reporters had put away his pencil and was outside when someone told him that Harry's son was delivering the eulogy. He made it inside to catch just a few words, but was lying in wait for the exit procession to get a quote from me.

"Did you call your father a 'Renaissance man,'" he asked. I told him I was on my way to the interment and that he could read about the eulogy in the papers. "But I'm from the *Ledger*," he said.

"Good. You'll be able to read it firsthand," I said as I got in the car and drove away.

Anne Sexton's words came back to me: "It doesn't matter who my father was; it matters who I remember he was." And I have chosen how I shall remember him.

# MEMORIES OF CATS AND OTHER STRANGERS

"Do you mind if we join you," said the New Yorker as he and his wife pulled the chairs back from our table. Whether I minded it or not they were there seated across the table, imposing their conversation.

I was hoping to enjoy the view of Lake George over my breakfast of black coffee and a bagel, but they interposed themselves on this fine September morning and civilly commanded my attention.

The darkly dressed woman, with long beads intermixed with an assortment of silver icons denoting her richly diverse spirituality, said that they were worried about the cats in their Manhattan apartment. I forget the number, but I remember them as extended family. I suggested that the woman give them a call. Perhaps she could talk to her plants as well and ease her anxiety. She laughed and said that she had already done so.

It has been forty years since that brief exchange—an insignificant moment in the life of the world, an obscure fragment of my personal history. It meant nothing at the time and it means nothing now. However, it is embellished forever in my memory banks and recorded for all eternity in some cosmic consciousness.

I will never know if our paths will cross again, perhaps pumping gas together at the same gas station in Georgia, or passing each other in the Louvre. Should we engage each other in conversation in the future, we shall never know of the last time that we spoke. I cannot say to everyone I meet, "Did we once speak of cats forty years ago?"

If I can believe that at some future time on the other side of eternity when all spirits merge into the Oneness of All That Is and there be united with those we know intimately and those we know only as passing shadows, then there is significance for our ephemeral dialogue about cats. Perhaps I shall also remember the young girl who sat next to me on a hill at sunset when I was seven, whose name I never knew; or the Egyptian who sold me a scarab in Aswan; or discussing Sartre's *Being and Nothingness* with a truck-driver over a hot dog and soda at the side of the road on a torrid August afternoon; or a thousand others with whom I have brushed shoulders at some time in our common journey through life.

There are no accidents in our casual encounters, whether an incidental act of kindness to a beggar on the street, or the road rage of an impetuous driver angered by your slower speed. It is the accumulation of these events over a lifetime that transforms us. The brief conversation that is seemingly meaningless and soon forgotten may at a deeper level of our consciousness have some ultimate significance. If so, then every encounter is meaningful and every person a part of the soul of God.

# PASSING SHIPS

*"Ships that pass in the night, and speak each other in passing;*
*Only a signal shown and a distant voice in the darkness;*
*So on the ocean of life, we pass and speak one another;*
*Only a look and a voice, then darkness again and a silence."*

—Henry W. Longfellow, Tales of a Wayside Inn

Longfellow's image of "ships passing in the night" caught the right mixture of human loneliness and alienation, like Edward Hopper's "Nighthawks" stopping for a cup of coffee in a desolate restaurant. Pools of faint light in deep darkness have a way of emphasizing isolation like stars on a cold night. The points of light do not connect, but the ancient peoples made the mental connections to form constellations and placed their heroes in the heavens. As we project our imagination into the night sky, so we may carry our loneliness and despair within us and project it onto our experience.

I would often make the commute from college to home late at night. It was a three-hour trip from Ursinus College in Pennsylvania to Newark—turnpike most of the way. The monotony of driving was relieved by the occasional stops at the Howard Johnson restaurants, an illuminated oasis in the darkness. I stopped there, not just for the coffee and a rest break, but for some human contact and reassurance that the species did not become extinct within the last hour.

Somewhere near Philadelphia I made a ritual of stopping at a particular HJ. The waitress on the midnight shift was pleasant enough, with a face that was more handsome than beautiful and eyes that conveyed deep sadness. She spoke with a French accent. I was fascinated by her, even though she was at least fifteen years older than I. It was the loneliness of the hour and the melancholy of her features that elicited my own feelings of alienation from the world and the deep need to be with someone.

Youth is an awkward age. Like fledgling birds pushed out of the nest, you either drop to the ground to be devoured by predators or you take off to explore your own worlds and find your own learning experiences. Growing up on Newark's east side, one did not come by the social graces easily. The conversation of teamsters and longshoremen was hardly a model for mobility in the worlds of academia and theologian-philosophers. I had to remind myself that Jesus hung out with coarse Galileans whose language was mocked by sophisticated Pharisees, and his association with prostitutes, sinners, and the dregs of society was often the source of scandalous rumors. Where a person comes from does not necessarily determine where he is going.

"What would you like?" she asked. I thought of a hundred possible answers that would have opened dialogue—or get me a slap in the face. I settled for simply, "Coffee, please." I wished I could have spoken French. When she brought the coffee, I said, "Merci." She smiled and walked away. It must have sounded like "Mercy," and perhaps that was what I really wanted.

She knew that I knew that she was French, but I didn't have enough of an accent to impress her. Henry Higgins was right when he said that the French don't care what they say as long as they pronounce it properly. In French, it's not only what you say but how you say it.

As the year passed I began to learn a bit more about the French waitress. Our encounters were limited to recognition and menu selections, but I would overhear bits of conversation with her co-workers and with truckers who also made routine stops. She was a war bride who came to America with a young GI she met during the occupation, but who had tired of her and left her for someone else. Now she was just trying to get by and find a new beginning. I knew she would. She was tough, resilient, and attractive enough. I wished at the time that we could have developed enough of a conversational relationship that I could have offered her a few words of comfort and encouragement without sounding intrusive. But we were only passing ships.

I sometimes think about people I meet in chance encounters—who they are, where they are going, what has become of them. A man I sat next to on the BMT train in New York twenty years ago frantically going through his briefcase looking for some missing papers. A woman making a remark about how her husband would kill her for her extravagant shopping spree and giggling about it between her expressions of worry. The cherubic child looking pensively out of a window on a cruise ship while her playmates were enjoying each other's company. Where do their lives take them from these brief moments when our lives approach one another but do not intersect? Does our brief exchange of words have any impact on altering directions, either by planting seed thoughts or by creating enough of a pause in a flow of thought to allow the consideration of new idea?

At Ebbets Field, long ago, I remember a ball boy gathering baseballs and tossing them into a big tub. The balls, covered in tough leather, some nicked and bruised by extensive play, rested against each other in the container, touching each other at only one point on the surface. How much like those balls we are, touching each other's lives briefly at some singular point in time, and only superficially. We never get to really know one another. But somehow, in the vast universe of God's love, we are a part of a greater whole, and there may be a design and intent in our seeming chance and brief encounters.

# "I WILL ALWAYS HAVE PARIS"

THERE ARE THOSE WHO define nostalgia as the longing to return to a time that you never lived in, but perhaps remember as though you did. In Woody Allen's film, *Midnight in Paris*, Gil Pender suddenly and mysteriously finds himself transported back in time to the Paris of the 1920's. This was a magical period in French history and I, too, would welcome the opportunity to chat with Hemingway, Fitzgerald, "Tom" Eliot, and other writers of the so-called "Lost Generation."

Our memories are a synthesis of our experiences. It is not only the sights and sounds of a time and place that we have lived through, but also that which has fed our soul through literature, film, art and music, conversation, and other nuances of the mind. I have created my own reality based upon my own images and preconceived notions.

I cannot recall my expectations when I landed at Orly for the first time. Was I thinking of Edith Piaf singing "La Vie en Rose," in some small nightclub on La Rue Pigalle, or Gershwin's *An American in Paris*, or an intellectual discussion with Albert Camus or Jean-Paul Sartre in Saint-Germain des Pres? But in retrospect, it didn't matter what Paris was; it mattered how I remembered it.

Paris is a city of love and romance. One goes to Paris not only to visit the Louvre or make the excursion to Versailles or enjoy the view from the Eiffel Tower, but to sample the French cuisine, browse the book stalls on the quays, stroll down le Champs Élysées, or have a glass of Bordeaux at one of the many sidewalk cafes. It is a place to fall in love or to remember the time when you were in love.

I didn't have much money in the sixties. As I walked down La Rue Monge I would stop at a store to buy my lunch: some fresh-baked French

# THE DWELLING PLACE OF WONDER

bread, a bit of *fromage*, and a bottle of wine. A bottle of wine cost about ten cents compared to a bottle of Coke which was more than a dollar. A bench in the small park nearby was a good place to experience the Parisian ambiance—the traffic in the street, the pedestrians who walked at a much slower pace than those in Manhattan, the two lovers on the grass in back of me.

The streets in Paris can be impossible to traverse. One sometimes must use the greatest ingenuity or sheer strength to make one's way across town. I was on a bus with some students as the driver tried to negotiate a turn at a small intersection. The problem was that a Renault was parked on the corner. After a few minutes of waiting for the car owner to finish his shopping, I recruited eight or nine of my fellow passengers who quickly lifted the small car and set it on the sidewalk. As our bus made the turn we could see the owner emerge from the store, looking very much confused. It would never happen in New York.

Paris was indeed the "City of Lights," and looking out over the Seine from the Eiffel Tower at night was unforgettable. It was iconic. It was like a huge time machine that transported me back to nineteenth century France when Gustave Eiffel constructed the entrance to the 1889 World's Fair. The tower was not without controversy, being condemned by the literary and artistic community, who compared it to a useless giant black smokestack obscuring all the revered Parisian monuments. And yet it has become the global symbol of France and no one thinks of Paris without the image of the Eiffel Tower.

Paris was where I had always wanted to be and where I hope to one day return. Ernest Hemingway wrote: "If you are lucky enough to have lived in Paris as a young man, then wherever you go for the rest of your life, it stays with you, for Paris is life, it is a moveable feast."

There are many periods of French history that I would like to visit, but, like Gil Pender in *Midnight in Paris*, it is the Paris of the 1920's that I would find most fascinating. Prior to the Great War, the forty year period known as *La Belle Époche*, "the Beautiful Era" was a time of peace and prosperity, a time of *joie de vivre*. It was during this period that Moulin Rouge and the Folies Bergere opened. Literary realism and naturalism flourished, which sowed the seeds of modernism. Writers associated with this period were Guy de Maupassant, Émile Zola, Marcel Proust, André Gide, Anatole France, Alain-Fournier, Paul Bourget, and the notorious and decadent Colette, whose sexually explicit "Claudine" novel series shocked even the French.

## "I WILL ALWAYS HAVE PARIS"

Growing up in an era of jazz and rock and "doo-wop," opera was in another world, often the subject of ridicule and mockery by the guys who sang on the street corner. My first exposure to a real opera performance was in Paris and the *Palais Garnier,* home of the Paris Opera. Puccini's *Madama Butterfly* would be presented, but without the superscripts that would become popular decades later. I was impressed. That is, until I spoke with the familiar character seated in front of me. The British actor, Robert Morley, was fidgeting in his seat, looking quite distressed. During the entracte, I introduced myself as a student visiting Paris and the opera for the first time, and I was presumptuous enough to offer to buy him a drink. He graciously declined and said that the performance of *Madama Butterfly* was the worst he had seen and then abruptly left the opera house. But I couldn't tell good opera from bad opera and took my seat to absorb the ambiance and excitement of being in this fine example of early *La Belle Epoche* architecture.

*La Belle Epoche*, and the American equivalent, the Gilded Age, ended with the assassination of Archduke Franz Ferdinand in Sarajevo in 1914, and the beginning of the Great War. World War I became the greatest cataclysm in the history of civilization to that point, and the generation born in the last decade of the nineteenth century was radically altered. The millions of deaths, the loss of values revered by the previous generation, and a sense of alienation and disillusionment had an impact that the world had seldom experienced. The war became known as the Grand Illusion, which became a film by Jean Renoir.

In fact, this generation became skeptical of all authority, adopting its own set of values and mores so very different from that of their elders. It was this rebellion that caused many of this generation to leave the countries of their birth in order to create a new social order. The phrase "Lost Generation" was used to describe the writers who left the United States after the war, disenchanted, lost, and searching. Many came to Paris during the 1920s to escape the memories of their past, but in Paris they were to represent the spirit of a new age.

Gertrude Stein is credited with using the term "Lost Generation" when she heard her garage mechanic referring to his hopeless assistant. She said to those who gathered in her salon:, "All of you young people who served in the war. You are a lost generation . . . You have no respect for anything. You drink yourselves to death." Ernest Hemingway liked the term and used it in his book, *The Sun Also Rises*. The Lost Generation writers circulated throughout post-war Europe, but were especially concentrated

# THE DWELLING PLACE OF WONDER

in Paris. They tended to write about disillusioned men who had lost hope and faith in contemporary society.

However, their writing styles differed. Hemingway, the macho, action-oriented writer, tended to use short sentences. His novels moved quickly without much reflection. He felt that omitting key events strengthened the story because it allowed the reader to fill in the blanks. Fitzgerald and T. S. Eliot, on the other hand, used symbolic imagery and allusion, with greater reflection.

F. Scott Fitzgerald's work, particularly *The Great Gatsby*, reflected his own hedonism and the consequences of a dissolute lifestyle. Just as Jay Gatsby's dissolute lifestyle resulted in his inevitable tragic death, Fitzgerald's own partying, carousing, and vast consumption of alcohol resulted in a heart attack at the age of forty-four. In a sense, *The Great Gatsby* is somewhat prophetic.

While in college I had read Bud Schulberg's book, *The Disenchanted*, the story of a disillusioned young writer, patterned after Fitzgerald, who sinks into an alcoholic morass. It was this feeling of hopelessness that embodied much of the Lost Generation writers.

Years ago, as a teenager, I was browsing in a used book store and noticed a section on "Southern Writers." I knew what Westerns were, but what were Southerns, and why wasn't there a Northern Writers section? I soon learned why. Here were books by William Faulkner, Katherine Anne Porter, Thomas Wolfe, Robert Penn Warren, Tennessee Williams, Flannery O'Connor, Carson McCullers, and many others. I began to sample these authors, especially Thomas Wolfe and Tennessee Williams. I eventually wrote my master's thesis on "The Secularization of Damnation: The Meaning of Existence in the Works of Tennessee Williams."

But it was Thomas Wolfe that got my attention that summer. Not officially a Lost Generation writer, he nevertheless wrote during the twenties and made a couple of trips to Paris during that time. But he reflected the spirit of the times. The major difference was that he still had hope and recognized that we can't go home again because the home we knew isn't there any longer.

We learn much from the brief moments of our lives when we are observant to the truths that we accidentally or unintentionally discover. Paris, like Camelot, was a brief, shining moment in my life, but it made a difference. As the best teachers are those who show you where to look, but don't tell you what to see, so I have learned from the details of my life. The true

## "I WILL ALWAYS HAVE PARIS"

artist paints not only what he sees with his eyes, but what he sees with his soul. We write not only about what we experience, but what that experience means to us. Why should we live if we are only going to accumulate the telemetry of life without interpreting it? We need those times of magic and wonder to just savor the experience and then later in life to reflect on what it means. That's why we will always have Paris.

# THE GLOAMING

THE EARLY CELTIC PEOPLES have always had a great respect for the natural world. They saw God in rocks and trees, in animals and flowers. Their world was filled with spirits, elves, fairies, leprechauns, and other creatures that inhabit the middle earth between the familiar and the magical, between our physical world and the spiritual realm. Their religious leaders, the "vision-poets," were able to see beyond our dimension into the spiritual world. They recognized that there are "thin places" in life when the veil between our normal existence and other worlds becomes so transparent that we can see beyond our limits of sight and sound.

Certain persons—shamans, priests, and others—had the power to walk between worlds, or at least bridge the gap between the natural and the supernatural. The high priest of the ancient Romans was known as *Pontifex Maximus*, the chief "bridge builder" between humans and the gods, between the physical and the spiritual. When Christianity superseded the Roman pagan worship, the title passed to the bishop of Rome who is still called the "Pontiff."

The thin places were not only locations in space, but also in time. It was the time of day that the Celts called the "gloaming," or dusk. It was a transitional time between the activities of the day and the quiet rest of evening as one consciously put aside the tools of labor and engaged in the more difficult work of caring for one's soul, of tending to relationships, of embarking on voyages of fantasy and exploring the landscape of dreams.

I learned from my grandmothers, Angelina and Natalie, how to use this thin time, for both had different ways of searching for meaning in their lives and coping with the problems that they faced.

# THE GLOAMING

Angelina Serio was not a very good cook and left the preparation of the evening meal to her daughters. While they were busy in the basement kitchen I would sometimes see her in the living room illuminated by the fading light of day filtering through the closed venetian blinds. At six o'clock every evening she would pause to say her rosary, tightly fingering the black beads and silver crucifix in a ritual act of devotion that went back centuries. There is an old-world tradition of the ringing of the Angelus bell at 6:00 a.m., noon, and 6:00 p.m. when the world would stop for a moment and remember the presence of God. The Angelus was a prayer commemorating the Incarnation—God with us, in the shadow times as well as in the bright hours of life.

Jean-François Millet's painting of "The Angelus" depicts two peasants at prayer in the field as the light fades. In the distance is a church spire and one assumes that the Angelus bell has sounded. Salvador Dalí, who lived in his own surrealistic world, thought that the man and woman were praying over their buried child, and indeed an x-ray of the work revealed the shape of a coffin beneath their feet. How appropriate to remember God's presence when we seem most abandoned by God.

When I received word that Leonard, a parishioner and friend, was diagnosed with cancer and had only a few weeks to live, I went to see him. Leonard had left the church a few years earlier and I had lost track of him. He hadn't joined another congregation, nor was he receiving the care and support that he needed in this transitional phase of his life. He was not married. He had no family. He was alone.

I sat with him many afternoons as we watched the fading light. Most of the time we said nothing. It was a ministry of presence. In knowing that someone was with him during these closing moments of this life was enough. We both felt closer to God and that God was closer to us.

At one point Leonard asked me, "What happens when you die? I've never done this before."

He asked me as though he really expected me to know the answer, as though I had experienced death before and remembered enough about it to tell him what to look forward to, as though there was some easy way to die or some pitfalls to avoid. "No," I said, "You just die the way you want to, and let God take care of the rest."

Leonard wasn't asking about what will happen to those he left behind, or his house, or his possessions. He wanted to know how he would die. What will happen to his awareness of life?

He looked at me intensely with his deep sunken eyes while I tried to find the words that would help him understand. I remembered all the metaphors that were used to help children grasp the meaning of death, of the bug that climbs the stalk and emerges out of the slimy pond to become a dragonfly, or the chrysalis that must change its form in order to survive in a new world.

I finally asked him what he sees when he is asleep. He said that every time he was asleep he felt that his dreaming was becoming more lucid. I said that as he moved in and out of consciousness, or the awareness of self, he would discover that what he had considered his unconscious was becoming more brilliant, more defined, more comfortable, as though this spiritual dimension was his normal state. He would also find that his awareness of this life would become more dreamlike.

The old hymn, which he knew by heart, but which he hadn't sung in years, brought some measure of comfort: "Abide with me, fast falls the eventide." God would abide with him when evening comes and "earth's joys grow dim, it's glories fade away." He will cross the river of forgetfulness and remember again what he had forgotten before he was born.

Leonard asked me to read Jane Kenyon's poem, "Let Evening Come" at his funeral. It seemed to fit his life, which had been one of much activity and interest in many things; but it was now time to let the natural course take its way. Kenyon, who died of leukemia, knew it full well when she wrote, "Let it come, as it will, and don't be afraid. God does not leave us comfortless, so let evening come."

Angelina's quiet mysticism in the gloaming of the passing day when she acknowledged the spiritual dimension of her life helped me to understand that we are much more than we think we are. There is a life being lived beneath the surface of this life. We can explore it in those thin times when we consciously seek the unconscious and simply let God be God to us.

Natalie Wertz used her gloaming time in a slightly different way. Between 4:00 and 5:30 p.m. she too would retreat into her living room, but not for prayer. Her ritual was listening to the afternoon soaps on the radio: "Stella Dallas," "Young Widow Brown," and "Backstage Wife." It was her way of moving from the reality of her day-to-day existence into a fictitious world of someone else's creation. We smiled when she said that it was time for "my story," but it really was *her* story. Her fantasy, her escape from the hard routines of her life, became her story, her means of coping with the world and her family.

Children live between the "long ago" and the "not yet," between the "once upon a time" and the "when I grow up." We create our dwelling places of wonder in the hidden recesses of the mind, places of refuge and escape when living in the physical world becomes too difficult for us.

Katherine Paterson wrote her best-selling children's book, *Bridge to Terabithia*, as a way of explaining to her son the sudden death of his friend, Lisa, who was struck by lightning while vacationing with her family. Children do not always comprehend the tragedies of life as they live through them, but they understand myth because they can view it from a point of refuge and safety. The bridge is perhaps the most important feature in any story—that which connects who we are to what we envision ourselves to be. It is in the envisioning that we fabricate our own methodologies in dealing with the world.

While the social life and affairs of celebrities in the forties and fifties never appealed to me as it did to Natalie who listened to her soap operas, I can understand today's fascination with the Kardashians and other celebrities, the people who are "famous for being famous." By vicarious participation in the lives of others, we either hope to avoid dealing with our own problems or we hope to find solutions to our own dilemmas. I would prefer to view it as a temporary disconnect to give us a bit of necessary respite.

We often live in shadowlands, that realm between sunlight and moonlight. The time of gloaming is a harvesting of light, much as the Jewish mother who lights the Sabbath candle uses the ritual motion of gathering the light so as to be a blessing to all who dwell within her home. So, too, Jews who gather for worship at sundown on Fridays greet one another with the words *Shabbat shalom*, or "Sabbath peace." Shalom also means "wholeness," "completion." We are never completely whole unless we have those down times, those sabbaticals of the spirit.

An old Scottish folksong speaks of "smooring" the fire, of putting out the hearth flame when night has come, much as the term "curfew" comes from the Old French for covering the fire. It was a time when the world acknowledged its need for rest.

I was just entering my teens when I heard a professor on "Sunrise Semester," a television program geared to academia, read Thomas Gray's "Elegy Written in a Country Churchyard." The opening lines resonated with me—"the curfew tolls the knell of parting day," and "leaves the world to darkness and to me." The Serios were nocturnal, and I had become acquainted with the night, finding it to be the most creative time of day and the most productive. Twilight was a time of quiet anticipation when the rhythms of life slowed enough for the mind to catch up and process the events of the day and of the world. I cherish the gloaming and its bridge to another dimension of being.

# ON BRADLEY CREEK

WE NEEDED THIS BREAK. This vacation. This time away. We needed to vacate—our house, our routines, our jobs, the people that we see every day.

The British call it "going on holiday." In a sense these are holidays (holy days), sabbaticals of the spirit as well as the body. We needed time for renewal and reflection.

Above all, we needed to get away from the incessant demands of caring for Mary Ann's ninety-two-year-old mother whose perception of reality differs remarkably from that of everyone else. Several years ago Mary suffered a number of strokes, which left her with reduced mental capacity and diminishing rationality. After a heart attack almost ten years ago and a ruptured pericardium, the doctors said that it would just be a matter of time. Well, everything is a matter of time, just like everything is within walking distance if you have the time, as Stephen Wright points out. Many years ago when a doctor told Mary Ann's son, Bill, that his smoking and drinking were bringing about a slow death, he told the physician, "That's okay. I'm in no hurry." He expected to outlive his mother, but unfortunately it was not meant to be. After Bill's death, Mary just faded into a shell of her former self.

Earlier in the week before we left for North Carolina, Mary, in her dementia experiencing a different reality, attacked the front door with her cane. She managed to undo the latch and made it down to the end of the driveway before I discovered her escape. Once on the sidewalk there was no way short of force to get her to return to the house. Attempts at reason, cajolery, pleading, and threats to call the ambulance were to no avail. She was intent upon stopping all traffic—pedestrians, bicyclists, motor vehicles—to enlist whatever help she could get. I stood a little way off to watch the tragicomedy unfold while I tried to think of a reasonable course of action.

Mary didn't know what she wanted, only that she wanted help in getting away. I explained to neighbors and persons out for their evening stroll that she was looking for a way to get back to Hungary. No one appeared interested in giving her a lift and her frustration grew, especially as she watched me casually conversing with her would-be rescuers. Finally, with the help of a kindly woman who seemed to have a way with caring for the elderly, we escorted her back to the house where she entered one of her catatonic states.

Her medication had been increased to limit these incidents. We had been reluctant to put her into a nursing home, regarding that as a form of abandonment and believing that people should be able to live out their lives in familiar environments surrounded by those who love them. But I had also seen many elderly parents outlive their children, wearing them out with their demands upon their love. Guilt can be a powerful motivator. It is not our custom, as among some of the Eskimo peoples, to allow the elderly to walk off into the wilderness and out of the lives of those whom they have nurtured. If we are the vessels of God's spirit, why is it so difficult to see the divine in the worn out shells of elderly humans? That spirit is still present and still teaching, and it's a hard lesson to learn. Our wise teachers still teach us, but not in the words that they once used.

When my brother-in-law Bill died, his son, Alan, sold his house in Wilmington. For thirty years we had been coming down to North Carolina and Wrightsville Beach. Now that the children were grown, it was just Mary Ann and I that made the trip. In recent years, Bill had come north to care for Mary while we took over his home. We would spend some time on the beach, visit antiquarian bookstores and antique shops, but mostly just rest, read, and write—and catch up on some serious talking that somehow managed to elude us for most of the year. We were amazed at how long the pauses had grown in our conversation, as though all the words had been spoken and that what we really need to say to each other was beyond the capacity of words. Just being with one another seemed to be enough.

With Bill gone, we were prepared to bring to a close this North Carolina portion of our lives. How delighted we were when Alan said that he had bought a town house on Bradley Creek. Since his job requires him to be in the Pacific tending to the Asian market, his company provides him with accommodations in Hong Kong. He comes back to Wilmington as often as he can, but he is frequently gone for months. He gave us the use of his place, and so the tradition continues.

Alan's house is a typical yuppie residence with five levels. One has the feeling of being in an Escher print, with people constantly moving either up or down. We can use anything we want in the house, he said, but not the Porsche. Not to worry, it isn't my style.

It is the view from the patio that has the greatest attraction. I love to sit there each evening and watch the world change from bright colors to darker hues of green and blue, penetrated occasionally by flashes of white boats and white birds darting horizontally across the frame of my view.

In the foreground are the shrubbery and mulch which the landscapers arranged along the trimly manicured footpath that leads to the boat dock. The marsh grass separates the hard ground from the water, but at low tide it is an oozy black gunk with an iridescent sheen from the microscopic specks of oil that wash in from the pleasure boats that make their way to and from the marina. It serves as a natural filtering system to keep Bradley Creek relatively clean and clear. The water shimmers in the fading sun, sending ripples of light and dark against the grass and the dock. On the distant shore is more grass and the dense entangled trees that serve as a forbidding barrier to Airlie Gardens.

A nearby pier protrudes a third of the way into the creek and ends in a floating dock that is perpendicular to the shore. Eight or nine boats of various sizes are moored there. I imagine Jesus of Nazareth standing on the dock on a Sunday morning and calling to those in the boats who are not thinking about the meaning of their lives but the pleasure of the moment. Nevertheless, it is a scene that belongs on canvas or digitally stored on a computer disk to be summoned back to memory in the bleakness of winter.

I wonder why this view appeals to my senses. Is the contrast between the natural world and the human intrusion upon it? Is it the subtlety of color, of peaceful hues of green and blue? Is it the slow movement of the water and the graceful flight of birds? It is calming to the spirit in ways that cannot be described.

Earlier in the day I sat on the beach. The morning was overcast and I was close enough to the water that if I looked out to a point above where surf and sand met, I could see no other differentiation between ocean and sky. They blended together in one drab shade of gray—no sea, no sky, no horizon. There was only the rhythmic pulsing of the breaking waves. How much we need contrast in our living, the valleys that make the mountains possible, the darkness that defines the light, the shadows that give shape and texture and meaning to the substance of life.

There are those who look for God in the natural world and see God's presence in creation. I see God also. God is the shimmering light upon the water; God is the path of a bird's flight, the gentle breeze that touches the cheek so briefly like an angel's kiss, the silence between the waves that remembers and anticipates. God is not so much in what I see, but in what God enables me to see. There is more to this world than I am able to perceive. There is more to life than my experience of it. There is more to being than merely existing. There is this magnificent astonishment of living to explore, for—to paraphrase playwright Robert Sherwood—this life, this theater of reality and the seemingly absurd, is indeed "a dwelling place of wonder."

# THE DWELLING PLACE OF WONDER

The comedian Steven Wright was asked if he had slept well. He replied, "Not exactly. I made a few mistakes."

How does one make mistakes while sleeping? We don't really, unless we avoid getting the deep delta levels that renew the body, and just as importantly, the REM stage where dreaming takes place. Dreams occur just below the levels of consciousness, and we drift into these stages four or five times during the night. Our dreams are necessary to process the events of the day, to make sense out of what is happening in our lives, to sort out what is important and meaningful.

During our awakened beta state and our relaxed meditative alpha level, measured by the amplitude of our brain waves, our senses are constantly being stimulated by vast amounts of data from the world around us, most of which we are not aware of. Our brains record all this sensory information—background conversations while waiting in line at the airport, visual images seen from the periphery of our sight as we cross an avenue in Manhattan, smells coming from a basement window of a restaurant in Chinatown—everything. Like a recorder on continual record, it is all there.

We need our dreams to sort it all out and make sense of what is important, what will affect our lives, our relationships, our future. We dream in images. Karl Pribram, neuropsychologist at Stanford who postulated the "holonomic brain theory of cognitive function," said that we think hologramatically and store our memories as holograms. Communication through written word and speech is linear and requires our brains to encode and decode what we say to each other.

## THE DWELLING PLACE OF WONDER

For this reason, we need allegory and myth to objectify our hidden hopes and fears, our loves and hates. We need to nourish the imagination of our children in order for them to deal with the vicissitudes of life. They need a place to which they can confine their monsters and a place where they can feel safe. If they are unable to find their havens in their homes or schools or churches or elsewhere in their physical environment, they will retreat to the hidden canyons of their minds and build their fortresses within.

J. R. R. Tolkien's *Lord of the Rings* and George Lucas' *Star Wars* are myths for our times. Like the great epics of the ancients—the Odyssey, the Aenead, the voyages of Jason, Sinbad, Brendan—they are more than simply adventure stories, but process stories about the search for meaning and fulfillment, the presence and influence of gods and demons in human affairs, redemption through undeserved suffering, the ultimate victory of the human spirit in the face of incredible adversity. They are also journeys of return, of coming back to the place where one has started, of coming home again.

Although I was only in Paris for a short time during my student days, the memories are vivid. We arrived shortly after noon from London on a BOAC shuttle and settled in at our hotel on La Rue Monge. I was looking forward to doing all those things that a young man in Paris is wont to do. The French have an expression, *cherchez la femme*, "find a woman," but I had no time for that. I was in love with the city itself. Mesmerized as I was by this enchantment, in my evening stroll along the quays by the Seine I noticed in the shadows two lovers locked in an embrace, oblivious to the fact that they had become an iconic symbol of what Paris represented—love, romance, youth, and the fading grasp of life.

A Kingston Trio song, "Raspberries, Strawberries," tells of an old man who returns to Paris later in life and finds that the winter winds blow cold and his dreams have turned to dust. But the memory is there, and it is the memory that keeps us alive and will shape our future. Ilsa was absolutely right when she said to Rick in *Casablanca*, "We will always have Paris." We live between memory and hope.

We come full circle in our lives only to begin again, to embark on a new journey. In his poem "Little Gidding" T. S. Eliot wrote, "What we call the beginning is often the end and to make an end is to make a beginning. The end is where we start from . . . the end of all our exploring will be to arrive where we started and know the place for the first time."

# THE DWELLING PLACE OF WONDER

I do not want to spend all my days looking at where I have come from. I look at my past in order to determine my future, even as my participation in the lives of friends and loved ones determines their destinies. As an ancient prayer states, "we are all together bound in this bundle of life."

But when memory becomes more important than vision, we stagnate and eventually die. We need to retain the wonder and imagination of our youth, to dream the dreams and see the visions, and move toward a future that we may not reach, but enjoying the journey every step of the way.